MISS TRUMAN TO SERVE

MISS TRUMAN
TO SERVE

With Best Wishes

Christine Truman

A MEMOIR BY
CHRISTINE TRUMAN JANES

Matador
Unit E2 Airfield Business Park,
Harrison Road, Market Harborough,
Leicestershire. LE16 7UL
Tel: 0116 2792299
Email: books@troubador.co.uk
Web: www.troubador.co.uk/matador
Twitter: @matadorbooks

Hardback ISBN 978 1803133 263
Paperback ISBN 978 1803133 270

British Library Cataloguing in Publication Data
A catalogue record for this book is available from the British Library.

Design, typesetting and production by John Haycock

Twin Zebra Productions 5 Strand on the Green London W4 3PQ
Telephone: 020 8987 8742

Printed and bound by CPI Group (UK) Ltd, Croydon, CR0 4YY

Matador is an imprint of Troubador Publishing Ltd.

Contents

Dedication

This book is dedicated to the late dear
Gerry, and to our children, Nigel,
Caroline, Richard and Amanda and
grandchildren Arthur, Morris,
George, Barnaby, Alice and Benji.

They have been proud, supportive
and delighted that I have made
this record for the family.

In memory of Mother, this book could
not have happened without her foresight
to keep my scrapbooks, photos and
every letter I received in my tennis
career. A wonderful collection to
look back on.

Acknowledgements

Writing my memoir would not have happened without support and encouragement from my family. They all took turns in typing my bad handwriting, which was not easy.

It was Terry Sheppey who stepped in to help. He patiently used his experience to show me the way forward. A constant source of encouragement in the background was Charles Woodhouse. From the start, he would not let me give up when I had many doubts. He read and re-read sections to urge me that I should keep going.

Lord John Grantchester has been a keen supporter, always showing great faith in my efforts to complete this memoir, which has been much appreciated.

Despite enjoying the project, it was often emotional reading through the correspondence that my mother kept which I had not seen. She would be thrilled to see the outcome.

Des and Rose Lynam have supported me all the way. It was Des who prompted me to put my memories down on paper. I am very grateful because it is a great feeling to have my tennis career recorded in my own words for the family.

There have been many willing helpers to lend an ear and more importantly read sections of my draft for feedback. They have always been optimistic and made me feel what I was doing was worthwhile.

In no particular order, I would like to thank Dr Michael Robson, John Inverdale, Simon Griggs, Sally Grant, Lucinda Heald, Craig Brown, Diana Hiddleston, Alex Palmer, Anne Sydenham, Sara Jenkins and Jenny Lloyd.

And lastly, good friend Sorel Mitchell. I mention Sorel last because it was her sister Sue and brother-in-law John Haycock who together took me over the finishing line. Without them, I am not sure where I would be now. Their experience has made my memoir happen. Thank you for all your hard work.

Milestones and Awards

1957   Wimbledon Ladies' Singles Semi-finalist, age 16
1959   Wimbledon Ladies' Doubles Finalist, age 18
1960   Wimbledon Ladies' Singles Semi-finalist
1961   Wimbledon Ladies' Singles Finalist
1965   Wimbledon Ladies' Singles Semi-finalist

1958   Pacific Coast Nationals Ladies' Singles Winner, age 17
       US Grand Slam Ladies' Singles Quarter-finalist, age 17
1959   Italian Championships Ladies' Singles Winner, age 18
       Swiss Championships Ladies' Singles Winner, age 18
       French Grand Slam Ladies' Singles Winner, age 18
       US Grand Slam Ladies' Singles Finalist, age 18
1960   US Grand Slam Ladies' Singles Semi-finalist
       Australian Grand Slam Ladies' Doubles Winner
       Australian Grand Slam Ladies' Singles Semi-finalist
1964   South African Championships Ladies' Singles Winner
       South African Championships Ladies' Doubles Winner
       German Championships Ladies' Doubles Championships Winner
       Italian Championships Ladies' Doubles Championships Winner

1957 – 1967   Played Wightman Cup for Great Britain
1963 – 1967   Played Federation Cup for Great Britain
1955 – 1977   Played County Week for Essex (Captain 1973-1977)

Awards:
1965   Received Sportsmanship Award
2001   MBE
2005   Honorary Doctorate, University of East Anglia
2011   Freeman of the City of London
2011   Voted 'Happiest Person in the Country'

Honorary memberships:
The All England Lawn Tennis and Croquet Club
The Queen's Club
The International Club of Great Britain

FOREWORD
by Des Lynam OBE

Lew Hoad and Ken Rosewall were in the men's final at Wimbledon the first year I really began to take an interest in events at the All England Lawn Tennis Club. There would be Australian domination for some years to come. The last British winner had been Fred Perry and there would be a wait of over half a century before Andy Murray came along. But things were looking brighter for Britain in Ladies' tennis, in particular we had the golden girl of the game, Christine Truman. Having already won the French Open title at the tender age of eighteen, she was now endeavouring to add the Wimbledon crown to her list of achievements. She was to be up against another British player in Angela Mortimer.

Christine's story takes us back to gentler times, when the game of tennis was still very much amateur, of wooden rackets, white tennis balls, when players didn't have the luxury of sitting down at changes of ends, when players didn't take on court enough equipment to supply Harrods sports department.

Her Wimbledon final earned her a voucher for £15 which had to be spent in the club shop. Nowadays she would have earned millions.

You will also hear about the physical impairment that she kept to herself during her years at the top of her sport, which might have prevented her playing at all.

I watched her play on our tiny black and white television but as things worked out, in due course she became my colleague at the BBC, and now I am very proud to be able to count her as a very wonderful and amusing friend.

I have just one regret when it comes to Chris. I never had the experience of meeting her redoubtable mother who once advised her daughter, one of the world's greatest players at the time to 'stop playing the drop shot, dear, it'll give you a mean face'. She must have been some lady. And Christine certainly is.

Introduction

LETTERS IN THE LOFT

I had not seen the correspondence that Mother kept during my tennis-playing days until four years ago. With Father working, and me away on the tennis circuit, Mother was left in charge of the post. This was the era when people wrote letters, and there were thousands of them. It was not possible for me to keep up with my mail in the short breaks I had at home, so Mother filed the letters in the year that they were written and kept them in sturdy boxes. During my married life, I moved house three times and each time those boxes moved with us. They were a precious cargo. Mother had left all my correspondence, scrap-books and pictures to the grandchildren in her will so they would not get lost. She also hoped I would read them myself, as she rightly suspected I lacked pride in what I had achieved in my tennis career. I promised I would, but it was always a case of next week, next month, or next year, as the task looked too arduous to tackle amidst a busy family life with four children under eight. Even now (I know I am slower!) it has taken me four years to complete the exercise, and it was a surprise how many goosebumps I felt along the way, and how much I savoured the fans' fervour which shone through in their written words.

Stepping back in life is not what I would ever do. I always look forward. But I was dumbfounded to discover how much people cared. It was a

Two triumphs for Royal Mail – and inspiration from a fan, written by a famous American writer and broadcaster

" And when the One Great Scorer comes
To write against your name,
He marks, not that you won or lost,
But how you played the game. "

Grantland Rice.

It occurred to me that you might possibly be willing to write a book of a short instructional nature aimed at the children's market. There are of course a number of instructional books aimed at adults but I don't believe that anyone has attempted to give an outline with the purely young player in mind. Such a book might I believe have a very considerable success and apart from the publisher who could be found without difficulty for the book rights, I think it is very possible that some newspaper might be interested in running it to co-incide with Wimbledon. If you felt that time did not permit you to involve yourself wholly in this project there would be no difficulty in finding a writer who would be able to work with you on it.

Our Client, Mr. Huntington Hartford, has particularly requested us to deliver to you the enclosed invitation to the Opening of Paradise Island.

Heartiest congratulations on your part in England's victory & on your splendid courage!

B. Ryland
(Suffragette ex-prisoner)

Part of a longer letter from a noted British literary agent. Even then, ghost-writers were available.

And three more extracts from the myriad letters in the loft

Would you take part in a Scrabble competition which takes place on the 24th October at Woburn Abbey - held there because of the Duke of Bedford's personal interest in the event. He is taking part. Scrabble is now a fashionable game and you probably know it; in case you do not, it is a word-making game, played crossword fashion, with a peculiar blend of skill and chance. It originated in the States, incidentally. Most people find it fascinating, if tantalising.

strange experience to look from the outside onto this person who was me. These letters were about my life, and now, here I was, stepping back to read about that person who was me in a setting long ago.

Famous signatures of Winston Churchill, Odette Hallowes the war heroine and a signed cartoon from Giles are timeless. Letters came from all walks of life: a fire crew; a nursing unit; a thank you from Borstal for a racket Mother must have sent; children wanting autographs; invites to film premieres and charity events, including an evening at Bertram Mills Circus that the Queen and Prince Philip were attending. It was a glamorous life, but I was still training and practising in my time off, so I could not have accepted many of these invitations. Let alone the many I never saw. One of those unseen invites I was sorry to miss was from Mr Huntington Hartford, the American billionaire and one of the richest men in the world, who asked me via his lawyers Gordon Dadds to join him on Paradise Island in the Bahamas for a tennis event. I can't believe I did not reply. Did Mother keep that one back? Doubt I could have gone without her.

Scrabble, my favourite board game, was another unseen request. I was invited to join the Duke of Bedford at Woburn Abbey for a Scrabble competition. He was apparently a keen player, and in October 1957 there was a trial to be held at Woburn Abbey to introduce this new game called Scrabble to Great Britain. I would love to have taken part but again, I was away and did not reply.

I regret that most of my mail remained unanswered, and it is amusing that those letters from the agents and publishers Curtis Brown, Michael Joseph and ILM, were each asking me to write a book. This was 60 years ago, and I have just replied, accepting their offers, but guess it is too late! Mother did her best, but my letters were an overload beyond her capabilities, and mine.

Since working with Des Lynam on the BBC Radio team, he always rings me on my January birthday and jokingly asks if I am writing a book yet. He told me many times I should write a memoir about tennis in the amateur era before it is too late. Tried not to think like that, but in January 2018, I took his advice, despite being warned that only the great Muhammad Ali can sell books on sport. Perhaps Emma Raducanu will join him soon? But the boxes of letters that Mother kept, gave me the impetus to record my story, as a memoir.

Chapter One

MISS TRUMAN TO SERVE

Despite the deafening ovation, I did not look up when I walked onto the Centre Court at Wimbledon for the first time. I had trained for years to reach this pinnacle, and now was my chance to tread in the footsteps of champions. I was not nervous. I expected to be here. Six rows back in the stands my family and coach were watching. The ball boys stood ready. The line judges waited by their chairs. Not a blade of grass was out of place beside the oh-so-straight white lines. The court looked small and more like a stage. The scene was set. The Royal Box was full. Now the match would start and I was ready to play. My first glimpse of reality was seeing my name on the scoreboard: Miss C C Truman. That's me!

That morning had started like many others. Back home at Woodford Green in north-east London, it had been breakfast as usual: cereal, followed by egg, bacon and fried bread. Mother had washed my lucky dress and my shoelaces, of course. I did not imagine anyone would notice my shoelaces on Centre Court, but that did not matter to Mother. She needed to know they had been washed. I slept well despite the tension of the coming quarter-final. All the daily papers printed an Order of Play for Wimbledon. This was the only way competitors knew what the schedule would be, so I sat tensely waiting with my parents for *The Daily Telegraph* to arrive. Turning to the sports pages, there it was in black and white: 'Miss C C Truman versus Mrs B Pratt.' I was due to play on Centre Court at 2pm.

Wow! But how did I get here? I have got ahead of myself. It was not only good fortune, but also a talent and dedication that were encouraged. I had a vivid imagination and an obsession with wanting to be good at tennis, not only to be better than my older siblings, but good enough to win Wimbledon. I must have been a pain, but these traits were nurtured by those who helped to steer me in the right direction.

No one does it on their own.

Chapter Two

BORN IN THE BLITZ

My childhood, by the standards of many, was unremarkable. Being born in the Blitz in January 1941 was not a problem for me, and my arrival as Number Five in the family was not a problem for Mother either.

A strong woman, Mother swore she took what nature sent her and got on with it. To be natural was important. Sex was never mentioned in our household. Being so young, I remember little of the war years. Not even Victory in Europe (VE) Day. Apparently for safety, Father evacuated the family to a cottage in Yorkshire, but we only stayed three weeks. I am told that when Mother saw a cow by the outside toilet, that was enough; we went straight home. She preferred Loughton in Essex and the bombs to country living.

At the age of four, I was taken to see the doctor because I was not talking at all. Mother was worried that the noise of the bombs had affected my hearing, but the doctor could find nothing wrong. Annoyingly for Mother, when I did start talking, I never stopped.

Unlike many town dwellers in the Blitz, we did not have an air raid shelter in the garden. To withstand the impact of a bomb, the downstairs of the house was shored up with wooden pillars, and the windows boarded over. Luckily, these precautions were never tested, and we escaped damage.

This was despite living in Loughton, which was under the bomber flight path to London. I have vague memories of being carried downstairs to sleep in the hall when the doodlebugs came over, and my eldest sister tells me I even had my own space in the cupboard under the stairs.

Life carried on for us. Schools stayed open and Father went to work, as usual, in the City. He was a chartered accountant with Sydenham, Snowden, Nicholson and Co. It was a pleasant surprise to find that the Sydenhams are now neighbours in Aldeburgh in Suffolk, where I live. Father's war job (most people had one), was as an Air Raid Precautions Warden. Before the war, the government had created this service of part-time volunteers, who also had full-time day jobs. They patrolled the streets to enforce the blackout, checking that no lights were visible to passing bombers. Their catchphrase, parodied by comedians during the war, was: 'Put that light out!' and it was a vital and often dangerous job. They saw the worst of the bombing and often were the first to help. You could recognise Wardens by their tin hats with a big 'W' on. As a family, we remembered Father in his hat, but sadly it was lost after the war. Food was rationed. Like many others we had no car or television set, and made our own entertainment.

Our main outing was going for family cycle rides in Epping Forest. This forest is a stretch of ancient woodland straddling the borders of east London and Essex. Like so many English forests, it was once a royal forest, with not just trees but woodland, grassland, heath, rivers, bogs and ponds. A wonderful place to be a child. I used to sit on a saddle perched on the crossbar of Father's bike. Sometimes we had picnics and picked blackberries. On one occasion, Father forgot I was still sitting on the crossbar when he got off the bike. Apparently, it was hysterically funny when I fell off, but not for me. Family humour.

At home we had a wind-up gramophone with a few '78' records. No doubt both the gramophone and the records are collectors' items now. There was a wireless, essential in wartime when everyone listened to the news, plus some books and board games. Mother would always be making something on her Singer sewing machine for us to wear, or she would be darning socks. Who darns socks today? Any family disputes were all dealt with by Mother. It did not matter who was at fault or who caused the argument, we were all sent to our bedrooms. It was surprising how quickly we became friends again.

In the summer of 1946, Father taught me his favourite game in the garden. It was not tennis. He picked up a pile of stones from the flower beds and put them in a bucket of water. I would wash them with soap, dry them, and put them back on the flower beds. Needless to say, this game took a long time, and Father said I was being helpful by cleaning the garden so well. A touch of the simple life.

No tennis rackets in sight. Yet.

It was a puzzle where the sports gene originated. I later discovered that there was a sporting relative on my mother's side. Although Mother was born in the UK and lived in Leytonstone, she was a quarter-Australian. She sometimes spoke about her relations, but they all seemed vague memories. After much research, extraordinarily it transpired that on 16th April 1809, The Reverend Robert Cartwright, Mother's great-great-grandfather, sailed to Australia aboard *The Ann* with his wife Mary, their five children, two maids and 198 convicts. The mind boggles to think that was possible. The journey took six months, which is also hard to imagine now. Robert Cartwright was the first colonial chaplain to receive a commission from King George III in January 1809. He had two older brothers, one of whom was an acquaintance of Horatio Nelson, with whom regular correspondence was exchanged. This was an astounding bit of history to discover in the family archives and I shall look differently at

Nelson's Column when I am next in Trafalgar Square.

After settling in New South Wales, Robert Cartwright's daughter, Jane, later married William Fowler in 1832. Their son William Jnr, born in 1843, was Mother's grandfather. He played cricket for Australia, and in 1862 he was selected to play against the first English Test team to tour Australia. Mother did remember these events, but never recognised any sporting connection with tennis 70 years later. Jane Cartwright had met William Snr on board *The Elizabeth* when she and her sister Mary were returning to Australia after a disastrous year at the School for Daughters of Clergymen, Cowan Bridge. They were enrolled in 1826 as pupils numbers 89 and 90. Whilst at Cowan Bridge, they met the Brontë sisters. These were not happy times. It was a harsh existence and the Brontës were equally struggling with the school's Dickensian regime. Maria and Elizabeth Brontë died not long after leaving Cowan Bridge. Jane and Mary Cartwright were quickly removed after only one year, suffering from poor health. *Jane Eyre* by Charlotte Brontë is thought to have included recollections of her Cowan Bridge days.

My grandmother Ellen Fowler, Jane and William Snr's granddaughter, was born in 1871. She took in 1900, what today would be considered a gap year, when she travelled to visit her married sister Charlotte in Leytonstone in East London. Ellen later married and also settled in Leytonstone where Mother was born.

When I was invited with Maria Bueno to tour Australia in 1959, I met Irene Fowler, a stepsister of Granny. She lived in Sydney, and had a room full of Cartwright-Fowler memorabilia, which she left to the Mitchell Library in Melbourne. Even though the meeting was pre-arranged, I think Irene was as surprised to see me as I was to see her. She had not married and was protective of the family archives. When she showed me some family heirlooms, I was not allowed to touch. Maybe she thought I would take them away! I regret not having more time to delve into our background. Tennis was obviously not part of any common ground, and unfortunately we both skimmed over what should have been an interesting conversation about the Fowler family history.

Father's background was more conventional in comparison. He went to Leytonstone High School and his studies were important. His parents were disappointed with any mark below 90% which was seen as a failure. In these current pandemic times, I am reminded that during the TB epidemic of the 1900s, my grandparents took in a young lad of 14, Harold Cooke, who had lost all his family. As Father was an only child, they thought Harold would be company. Harold never forgot this generosity and became a kind uncle to the Truman family.

After the war was over, our neighbours in Loughton found an old tennis net in their garage, and thought it might be useful for my older siblings to use in the garden. They knew my parents had enjoyed playing tennis before the war as they had met at Fillebrook Road Tennis Club in Leytonstone. After they married, their mutual interest in tennis had taken them to Wimbledon long before I came along. Stars such as Fred Perry, Suzanne Lenglen, Kay Stammers and Dorothy Round, among others, were champions at that time.

Father regretted never being encouraged to play sports as a boy in case he got his whites dirty. His schoolwork took precedence. Nor was he allowed to play games on a Sunday. None of us ever remember him changing this habit. He was not judgemental, but as Treasurer for 39 years of the local church, St Mary's in Loughton, it meant we had to go to church every Sunday morning, something I rebelled against in my teenage years. This somewhat spartan, independent approach manifested itself in many ways. Oddly, Greek was one of Father's favourite hobbies. He read what looked to us like thick boring books in Greek, but he enjoyed them and called our house, 'Makaria', which is Greek for 'Bless this House'. Not a Greek restaurant, as some passers-by thought! None of us remember Father ever helping with our homework, which would have been useful. Even his writing was an example to copy, despite him using a quill with a nib he dipped into an inkpot. He preferred playing hockey, football or cricket, whichever was our sport of the moment. Croquet was the only game Mother banned because it caused too many arguments. However, we were all happy to take on new sports and so the neighbours' tennis net was gratefully accepted.

A court was soon marked out in the back garden. It was on a slight slope with a path across one end. My four older siblings made an ideal family mixed doubles. Elizabeth, Philip, Humphrey and Isabel spent many hours playing together. I watched enviously, desperate to join in, but they told me to go away because I was not good enough. Not good enough? Nothing could have made me more determined than to be told I was 'no good' by my siblings. The family still laughs about it today. But when I look back, I am sure that this introduction to tennis was the reason for my future choice. All I wanted to do was join in and play with them. My only ambition was to play tennis as well as they did. However, being Number Five in the family, I was waiting in the wings and, like a coiled spring, I was ready to pounce. It was not an unhappy stage of growing up in a large family. I knew no different and expected to wait for my older siblings to go first. After all, I was four years younger than Isabel, the youngest in the family mixed doubles.

Mother always maintained that in a large family, the oldest and youngest were the most spoilt; the eldest having everything new, and the youngest having the best because they were last. As Number Five, I am still waiting for my own bike, before it's too late. Her other theory was never having to teach us how to catch a ball. According to her, we all had a natural hand-eye co-ordination from the age of two.

Despite not playing tennis yet, exercise was important to Mother. She took me and my sisters, Elizabeth and Isabel, to ballet and Greek dancing classes every week. These were popular pastimes for children and thought to be educational as well as fun. The highlight of this time was winning the book *Red Shoes* as a prize for passing a ballet exam. It was later made into a film starring Moira Shearer. Thank goodness I did not take up ballet, as I was going to be six-feet tall. My 'Pass' certificates for my Greek exams were signed by none other than Victor Silvester, the famous dance band leader. He was a judge, but I never met him or better still, saw him judging.

Swimming was another popular activity which I enjoyed. This was post-war and, in hardier times, it was not always tempting, as outdoor pools had no heating. My certificates record my number of lengths but not the water temperature of 9°C (49°F). Little did I know this was good preparation for swimming all the year round in the North Sea at Aldeburgh in Suffolk, 60 years later.

Me, aged three; with family pet on rocking horse. Hardly room for both of us!

L to R, at rear: **Philip, Mother, Father, Elizabeth and Humphrey**
and in front: **me, Nell and Isabel**

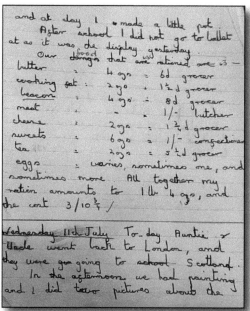

A page of homework, showing cost of rationed food and quantities per week which were allowed in 1951. A school photo, age 10

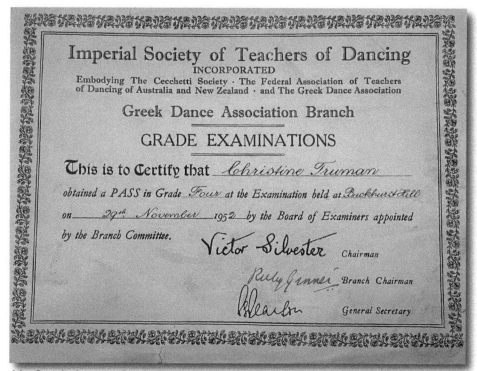

My Greek dancing Grade Four 'Pass', signed by Victor Silvester, the famous British band leader and dance instructor

Chapter Three

MOVING HOUSE

Regrettably, I never did play in the family four at Loughton because, when I was eight, we moved to 10 Snakes Lane, Woodford Green in Essex. Nell, my younger sister, had arrived five years after me and we had outgrown the house in Loughton. My tennis career started in the garden at Woodford Green.

Growing up in London in the 1940s and 1950s, it is hard for me to compare that world with today's. Woodford Green was a typical suburb. In the days before supermarkets and convenience stores, the milkman came every day with a delicious dollop of cream at the top of a pint of milk. Ration books allowed a small portion of sweets weekly. Every Saturday afternoon I went with Father to select our allowance. The sweet shop did not have many choices. I chose aniseed balls as they lasted the longest, although I did not like them that much. We had to get fondants for Mother which was disappointing as they took up most of our allowance.

Unlike the modern high street, full of shops with a fantastic range of fashions, there was the men's outfitters, and the haberdashery store. It was in Puddicombes, the haberdasher's shop in Woodford Green, that I was to buy my 'lucky' cardigans. Mother took me to choose the colour for the big occasions such as Wimbledon, from the limited selection on offer.

For me, 10 Snakes Lane had one distinct advantage over Loughton: half the old-fashioned house had a brick wall which backed onto a lawn. At last,

I had my chance to play tennis. I hit my first balls against the wall using Isabel's old racket. I hit and hit and hit. The lawn itself was the size of a singles court and, later on, this proved ideal for service practice and volleying. Father liked nothing more than to come home after work and hit me a box of tennis balls to volley. The lawn was too uneven for ground-shots. He put a cardboard box of 25 balls on the kitchen stool and hit the balls all over the garden. Father's shots, being unpredictable, certainly speeded up my reactions! This exercise today would be the equivalent of a coach having a basket of balls on wheels, or even a ball machine with a hundred balls or more. Our neighbours at 12 Snakes Lane later put a gate in their fence so we could collect all the balls that went in their garden. It was an amazingly kind gesture, never to be forgotten. On the other side, at 8 Snakes Lane, there was an old peoples' home, and they liked to watch me practising. Luckily, my balls did not make a direct hit on the spectators.

The period after the war was important for tennis. Clubs were developing all over the country, and Elizabeth and Father joined Monkhams Lawn Tennis Club in Woodford Green. They were followed in turn by Philip, Humphrey and Isabel, all of whom became strong players. My parents did not intentionally hold any of us back, but being Number Five, I still had to wait my turn.

As tennis became more popular, the demand for coaching grew. In Essex we had a well-known coach called Herbert Brown. He was not a famous player, but he had a wonderful knack for enthusing young players. My big breakthrough came when Isabel was ill, and could not go to her tennis lesson with Herbert Brown. I shared a room with Isabel and dreaded she might get better. I kept running up and down the stairs to make sure she was still ill. It was not sisterly, but her illness was a red-letter day for me. She did get better after a few days but, aged nine, I had my first tennis lesson because she could not be there.

From then on, I travelled each week with Mother to Wanstead, only three miles away, where Herbert Brown had his own tennis court. The lesson was for half an hour and I ran the entire time, hitting and picking up balls. Herbert's favourite ploy was to promise a new racket or a new box of balls, as a prize to aim for. The target might be winning a set or even four games, but he was good enough to let me get within reach of the prize and then step up the pace, and I always went home empty-handed. Believe me, I practised like mad before my next lesson. But it was always next time… next time…

Former pupils of Herbert Brown still ask me how many rackets I won, and are surprised to learn that I never won a prize. His coaching was based on a set of simple techniques. He did not pretend to be a coach of skills and tactics. For groundstrokes, I was to shake hands with the racket for my forehand grip, then make a small loop with my arm, while stepping forward to follow through and keeping my eye on the ball. He picked up on my habit of placing my forefinger along the racket handle and moved my hand slightly anti-clockwise to improve my backhand and service grip. His lessons were not wasted on technical discussions. Like most youngsters, I simply wanted to play. His main advice was: 'Hit the ball hard!'

He also kept an old racket for use as a 'throwing racket' to demonstrate the service action. Later, I was fascinated to learn that Richard Williams, father of the Williams sisters, kept a large basket of old throwing rackets on his porch for Venus and Serena to use for serving practice. In the film *King Richard*, he can be seen watching the girls throwing rackets and balls as a service drill. Herbert was ahead of his time. He became the best-known coach in Essex and taught many county and international players. I assume he must have persuaded my parents to allow me to take regular lessons because I never looked back.

In a period when rationing of food and materials was still in force,

Mother made my first tennis dress from pillow slips. Sheets were more difficult to buy than pillow slips. I was told sheets needed more tokens so pillow slips would have to do.

Being able to start my tennis career with an inspiring coach was extremely important. No one can be successful without support along the way. Coaching at the start of learning anything new avoids bad habits, which can be hard to change at a later date. Foot-faults come to mind. Even the slightest infringement can be hard to correct. Unfortunately, coaching can give tennis an elitist label. It costs money, and limits the numbers who might be able to play. I console myself by hoping that today no one misses out on an opportunity to hold a racket and try tennis, now that the Lawn Tennis Association is putting more resources into grass roots. It is important that not just future Wimbledon Champions are inspired, but encouragement is given to those who want an enjoyable hobby and like to take exercise socially with friends. Who knows, there might just be a friend of a friend who could become a champion of the future? I fell on my feet by having the right help at each stage of my career.

My first tournament was the Essex County Closed event at Traps Hill Tennis Club in Loughton. I was 10 years old and still running to pick up the balls between points. I thought this would give me more time for the match. I also did not know how to score properly, so the umpire had to tell me when to change ends. There were only two age-groups in most junior tournaments. These were Under 18, and Under 16. Naturally, aged 10, I was outplayed – but losing did not dull my enthusiasm; far from it, and I knew not to let any disappointment show for a very good reason.

Mother was strict; she had to be with six children. Her code of conduct was clear and strictly observed. Behaviour came first. From the start, I knew that if I showed any sign of temperament I would be taken straight off court and sent to my bedroom. Secondly, our whites had to be whiter-than-white. This included my shoelaces being washed. The result came third. She never wavered from this ethos throughout my career. People complimented me on my good behaviour. But until the age of 21, I honestly thought I would be sent to my bedroom if I did not behave. One look at Mother and you knew you had to get on with it.

Her sayings and superstitions were a constant reflection of her code. She would not let me go back for something I had forgotten. She believed that would be unlucky. Her favourite sayings were: 'A blind man on a trotting horse would be pleased to see anything.' 'Never judge a book by its cover!' 'A smile and a thank you costs nothing.' And the more sobering 'A bird in the house was a calamity.' Or if she dreamt of fire, it was a bad omen. And the most relevant to me: 'A good workman never grumbles with his tools.' She swore by Sanatogen to 'keep going', and would mix this white powder with a cup of tea or coffee. Should a guest say they were feeling low or under the weather, Mother would immediately make them a compulsory drink of Sanatogen. Red Label Petrolagar was her remedy for constipation. It was revolting and I can still taste that white substance today, but it worked! Lastly, Basilicon ointment was used for splinters and spots. These potions, of her era, were in the medicine cabinet as an answer to every ailment. I am not sure if they still exist, let alone work their magic, but she was pleased when she asked the chemist if her remedies worked. To which the chemist replied: "If you have faith, of course they work."

Luckily, my parents knew nothing about the technique of tennis. They had never had coaching. My matches were never analysed or talked about. Father used to say to the press: "Christine enjoys a game of tennis," as if it were a hobby. The only tactic Mother hated was the drop shot. She was adamant that this was a mean shot, and I would grow up with a mean face if I used a drop shot to win points. If I do have a mean face, it is not because I played drop shots.

In the garden at 10 Snakes Lane, Father's unpredictable shots speeded up my reactions; *right*: Serving, aged 10, in my first tournament at Trapps Hill Tennis Club, Loughton

Running to pick up balls, aged 10 in my first match at Trapps Hill Tennis Club; *and right*: Aged 13, with trophies

With all my siblings: Humphrey, Philip, Isabel, Elizabeth, me and Nell

Me, Isabel and
Humphrey

Chapter Four

BRAESIDE

In the early 1950s, family life was changing. My brothers and sisters, like me, were growing up and their futures beckoned. Philip had joined the Merchant Navy. Was he taking after Nelson? Elizabeth had gone to Anstey Physical Training College in Birmingham, a pioneer training college for teachers of girls' Physical Education. Humphrey and Isabel were nearing the end of their school days.

When my parents first took me to Anstey to see my sister Elizabeth, the Principal of the College met us for a friendly chat. She looked at me, aged 11, and asked: "What do you want to do when you grow up?"

I said: "I would like to come to Anstey, but only if I'm not playing at Wimbledon or in the Wightman Cup." She smiled at my precociousness.

Braeside School for Girls in Buckhurst Hill, Essex was a defining stage in my tennis career. For five years it played an important part in my all-round development. It was a chance decision which changed my school days.

Aged four, I had started attending Essex House in Woodford Green, a prep school which prepared pupils for the critical test faced by all British children; the 11+ exam. Unknown to me, Miss Huntley, the headmistress, suggested to my parents that Braeside might suit me better. She felt the strain of this exam was too much, so I left Essex House aged 10, as Braeside took girls from age five to 16, regardless of exams. This turned out to be the best move I could have made. Strangely, in those days, none of these decisions or problems were discussed with me at all. I remember visiting Braeside with my parents and liking the school, and that was it; off I went!

Surprisingly, I did pass the 11+ at Braeside in 1952. My siblings teased me saying: "They let a few duds through." This coincided with Churchill's election victory in 1952, and his promise that all British children who passed this exam would have their school fees paid for the remainder of their education.

To celebrate this news, my parents bought me my first new tennis racket. I still remember cleaning it every night. Although I now had a place at Loughton High School, I stayed at Braeside. Did my parents know that Miss Wakefield, the headmistress, was keen on tennis? That I will never know. But I do know that without her permission to have time off school to practise, my early success would not have happened. To specialise in a talent was thought a daring new concept, and it would never have been allowed at the High School.

This initiative was not to everyone's taste of what was acceptable. Out of the blue, I learned this at a farewell dinner party before we moved to Suffolk from Woodford Green, 22 years ago. Two of my former teachers were at the party. After the main course, one of these teachers from Braeside let slip the comment: "It was disgraceful that Miss Wakefield allowed you permission to have so much time off school to play tennis." This was a conversation-stopper among the party guests, as I was now 59, with four children. All I could think was, thank goodness this teacher was not my headmistress 48 years ago, but it made me realise there would be many others like her who thought the same.

Looking back, I think Miss Wakefield was ahead of her time with her decision to let me take advantage of my opportunities. It would be more acceptable today, as it is possible to weave a talent around the school calendar and continue combining these ambitions throughout university, either here or abroad. Colleges in the USA are renowned for their sports scholarships which are proving to be successful.

Braeside was the backbone of my early teenage years from 11 to 15. At 11, I already knew I wanted to be a Wimbledon Champion, and play in the Wightman Cup. It is hard to explain or describe what made me so single-minded. Of course, there were not as many sports on offer compared with nowadays. Maybe I would have been tempted by the many options currently available, from trampolining to martial arts, but my heart was set on tennis. I had a racket clip on my hand-me-down bike and cycled the half mile to Woodford Wells Tennis Club after school to practise. Often there would be no one to play with and I hit against the wall. Perhaps having once been told I was no good stayed in my subconscious, and drove me to practise no matter what. Mother now had more time to take me to tournaments, sometimes with Humphrey and Isabel. My ambition was still to be good enough to play with them.

Being at school gave me a normal routine. I made lifelong friends, loved netball, and my daily life was ordinary. My favourite school lunch was macaroni cheese followed by spotted dick or jam roly-poly. Hardly healthy options for an athlete, but delicious. Swimming lessons were at the outdoor Kingfisher Pool in South Woodford. We must have been hardy, as the temperature was often 9°C (49°F) at the beginning of the summer term. Our PE teacher, Mrs Harston, promised an Effort Point if we jumped straight in. Always keen to have a go, I jumped in off the diving board and got three Effort Points. This topped up my end-of-term Effort Point score no end.

People are often surprised to discover I did not learn to play tennis at school. This was not unusual. Braeside was not a sports school. Its facilities were sparse. There was a large garden and one netball court, which was also used as a tennis court in the summer term. The gymnasium doubled up as a dining room, with a few wall bars on one side. A gymnastic horse was kept in a cupboard along with a springboard with no spring. No one ever jumped over that horse, so our PE lessons were quite limited, netball not tennis, being our main focus.

When I was 11, the Braeside Sports Day took place on a field nearby. Teachers held a string across the finishing line for running races, while a whistle was blown at the start. With my long legs, my forte was the high jump. The apparatus was a basic bar supported by two upright poles. There were no mattresses for a soft landing. The scissors jump was the only known approach in those days; the Fosbury Flop, created by Dick Fosbury, an American athlete and Olympic Gold Medallist in 1968, came later. On damp grass (a stumbling block in the future?), I ran and slipped under the bar, breaking my left wrist. No one knew I had done any damage. When I complained that my wrist looked odd, I was just asked to move out of the way so the girls could finish the contest. Don't make a fuss. However, with my left arm in plaster, I was still able to play tennis and I entered the Woodford Wells Club Tournament, serving under-arm. I won, and received two bookends as a prize – a memorable win with a broken arm. Despite sports day, Braeside will always be a defining moment for me. By chance, fate dealt me the best cards.

In the autumn of 1952, my parents made me a junior member of The Queen's Club. This was a brave move, because Queen's was an hour's drive across London, yet it was the closest venue with covered courts and a chance for me, aged 11, to play tennis throughout the winter months. Today, indoor facilities are more commonplace, but every Thursday, after school, Mother drove me to Queen's for my lesson with Mr Pearce, a professional coach with a friendly manner and bags of enthusiasm. Herbert Brown was still my coach in Woodford Green, but with Mr Pearce I hit a lot of tennis balls during our hour-long lesson. Inspired, I thrived on this indoor advantage.

These trips were the highlight of my week. The covered court surface was wood, painted green, and not a surface I have seen since then. It was fast, and unheated. There was a single electric bar in the gallery. Wearing only my home-made dress and cardie, I ran around desperately trying to keep warm. Excellent for the footwork.

Mother sat through every lesson in the freezing gallery. Despite feeling cold, she wanted to watch and this was important. I can see now that having her in the gallery made every shot matter. The professionals today would never step on a practice court without their entourage for encouragement. The only time a lesson was cancelled was when the fog was thicker inside than out. Practising through the winter months certainly paid dividends. Now 12 years old, and growing tall, I had improved and felt more confident.

Wimbledon was still four years away, but Mother had won tickets in the Championships ballot for the 1954 men's final. She took me to watch. A 'wow' moment. It was an emotional final when the popular Jaroslav Drobny, considered old at 32, beat the young 19-year-old Australian, Ken Rosewall. Age is no barrier today. Jaroslav Drobny had defected from Czechoslovakia in 1949, aged 27, taking on Egyptian citizenship. He eventually settled in Putney, west London in 1959. Little did I know the part Drobny would later play in my career. Going home after watching the final, I felt excited and could not help but visualise myself playing there one day.

There were three important events that changed things for me in 1953. The first was being a bridesmaid to my eldest sister Elizabeth, in February. I was allowed to have my straight hair, which I hated, curled, and the perm gave me a mass of curls. But Shirley Temple I was not, and I never wanted curls again. Secondly, I was the cause of a family upset when I beat older sister Isabel in the first round of the Easter Essex Junior Tournament at Woodford Wells. This draw was unfortunate. None of the family came to watch, not even Mother. Maybe they sensed the outcome. Isabel had been a promising junior, but at 16 her interest in tennis did not match mine. She had more exciting interests off court, whereas my competitive streak was my strength. At 12, I won the U16 event, but I felt like a baddie in the family, and was unhappy that no one wanted me to win. It took some time for my success to be accepted. I was not supposed to beat Isabel. It was wrong. Eventually my siblings relented, and no longer laughed at my efforts to improve. They once would tease me for skipping before breakfast and going to bed at 8pm to make sure I had enough rest for my training. Hiding my wool for knitting tennis jerseys in the evenings was another 'family joke', but these disruptions were now accepted as part of my routine.

I knew times had changed when my siblings became valuable practice partners, which was a huge step towards my improvement. Finding people to practise with as a junior is never easy, so it was an advantage to have the bonus of family when they were at home. Now, aged 12, I was winning U18 events.

My third moment, and the most important, was my big breakthrough in *The Evening News* Tournament, an event just for the Home Counties, sponsored by *The Evening News* newspaper. The early rounds were played locally, with the semi-finals and finals being played on the grass centre court at The Queen's Club. It helped that I was already familiar with the Club, having been a junior member for nine months. Aged 12, I won the 12–15 event. It was my first major title. I won a black shield with my name on.

Unknown to me or Mother, Dan Maskell, the LTA professional coach, was watching me play. He was looking for potential juniors to join his LTA Training Scheme. Dan's role was to focus on the top handful of juniors in the country, with the best coaching available. It was a starstruck moment when he congratulated me and invited me to join his programme. This would mean having regular weekly coaching and practice from the LTA professional Dan Maskell at Wimbledon. An exciting reward for winning *The Evening News* Tournament and big changes ahead for a 12-year-old from Woodford Green.

Herbert Brown reluctantly agreed it was the opportunity I needed to move onto the next stage of my development. We remained good friends. Miss Wakefield, my headmistress at Braeside, was also delighted. Without her support, my LTA training with Dan Maskell would not have happened.

Dan Maskell was an impressive coach. We got on well from the start. Aged 12, I had a season ticket for the Tube from Woodford Green to Southfields, Wimbledon. I travelled in the last carriage where there was always a guard on duty who kept an eye on me, which gave Mother peace of mind. The journey took one and a half hours from door to door, quite a trek for a 12-year-old, but it was only twice a week to start with. Dan met me in his car at Southfields Tube station, so that I would not be late for my lesson. We drove from the station to the All England Lawn Tennis Club, where I walked into another world. Wimbledon here I come.

Practising with the Centre Court in the background was uplifting. Wimbledon became familiar, and it seemed possible that I might play there one day. On reflection, my familiarity with the grass courts was important. I was not intimidated by their perfection or the aura of playing on them. I would like to think that all youngsters have the chance to savour the atmosphere of the All England Club before they get to play there, rather than feeling daunted by the prospect. Sometimes, after my lesson, Dan would take me through the famous double doors that lead onto the Centre Court with Rudyard Kipling's inscription of 'Triumph and Disaster' overhead. Dan would let me walk onto the court itself. A goosebump moment. This is when Dan first said: "Christine, I want you to feel this grass beneath your feet – because one day you will play here."

Sitting on the Tube going home I could not stop thinking about walking onto the Centre Court and being allowed to stand on its famous turf. I wanted to believe it was true that Dan Maskell thought I could play there one day. His enthusiasm and optimism certainly spurred me on.

At last, Snakes Lane had a television. It was only small, with a black and white screen that was so fuzzy it was hard to see the ball. But I could now watch the Wimbledon Championships after school and try and imitate the best players, copying their winning strokes, and mimicking the champions. *Treasure Island*, a favourite book, had also arrived on TV but they did not clash.

Lottie Dod was my heroine. She had won Wimbledon aged 15 in 1887. I knew I could not emulate her record, as the age limit was now 16 at Wimbledon. But I always saw myself as a Lottie and wanted to be as good as her when I was young.

'Little Mo', the US star Maureen Connolly, was my other example. She won Wimbledon aged 17, 18 and 19. These players captured my imagination. There was an excitement about them achieving so much at a young age. It felt dramatic, although I would not call myself a dramatic person (not yet anyway). I found their youth motivating and invigorating. I aimed to be just like them.

Aged 12, with my first coach, Herbert Brown, having a lesson
at his home in Wanstead, Essex

Lottie Dod, my heroine

Very pleased with my new racket

Aged 14, with Ann Haydon, after losing to her in three sets in 1955 in semi-final of Junior Wimbledon

With Gillian Pears, when I won the final of *The Evening News* tournament at The Queen's Club in 1953

Getting ready to practise, aged 12

Winning the Junior Under-18 Indoor Championships at Queen's, aged 14

Chapter Five

A BREAKTHROUGH

After winning *The Evening News* event at 12 years of age, Dan Maskell hailed me as a future champion. For the first time in my life, I saw my name in the newspapers. Sports reporters wrote that I had a promising future. Steve Roberts from *The Evening News* wrote: "Britain has a new Little Mo. Her name is Christine Truman. She is 12 years and 7 months old – and tall. I have never seen a British youngster with such complete concentration, scarcity of nerve and supply of strokes." This publicity led to a phone call from the BBC. A producer from a Children's Hour panel game, hosted by Richard Dimbleby, rang Mother. The producer asked if I could appear at the BBC, saying it was £3 and 10 shillings.

Mother resisted. "Certainly not!" she said. "We can't afford that sort of money for Christine to appear on television."

It took a while and some persuasion, to clarify that the figure was not an entrance fee, but a payment for appearing on the programme.

I duly appeared and soon found out that a quiz on TV was not my forte. Richard Dimbleby showed me a picture of a Great Dane. I had to name the dog. I knew it was a Great Dane. I could see it was a Great Dane. But my brain flipped. When pushed to identify the dog, I said: "It's a Great Aunt." Poor Richard Dimbleby could only say he hoped I did not have a Great Aunt that looked like that.

When I was 13, Eamonn Andrews, better known as the presenter of the immensely popular *This Is Your Life*, a TV programme from 1955 to 1987, interviewed me on his programme *Radio Sports Highlights*. I had never thought of myself as a highlight, but Eamonn was a fun person, and at that age it was exciting to meet such a famous presenter who made me feel I actually was a highlight on his programme.

Sterling Henry Nahum, known professionally as Baron, the society and court photographer, invited me to a photo shoot at his smart London studios. Mother drove me to Pimlico in my brown raincoat and brown school tunic. I borrowed my sister Isabel's tennis dress. It was smarter than the pillow slips. Baron was charming. His only comment being: "Could you straighten your eyebrows?" I still think about my eyebrows today when I have a picture taken.

This was my first taste of sporting fame. The two Baron portraits hang proudly in the bedroom. I thought I had the originals, so it was a surprise to find my young self staring back at me in a pub quiz two years ago. Needless to say, I was the only one to identify them. It was my one contribution to my team. No one else recognised this 13-year-old.

Above all, at that age, I was still growing. I was taller than my parents, three sisters and one brother. Many times there were tears when I blamed my parents. I said it was not fair. Inside, there was always a 'little me' trying to get out.

At this time, there were no cash prizes in junior tournaments. Playing tennis was funded by my parents. Competition winners received a small cup, normally a replica of the official cup, or a shield, which could be kept. Occasionally, my parents promised me a prize if they thought I had done better than expected. This would be a jigsaw or a book token. Woodford Wells Club at the edge of Epping Forest was now our local club;

Monkhams Lawn Tennis Club having built houses on their six shale courts.

The Woodford Wells Ladies' Captain kindly included me, aged 13, in senior club matches. Although these were doubles, it was match practice against a variety of styles. Most of the team seemed to have injuries judging by all the strapping on view and, being the youngest, I had to do all the running and retrieving for my partners. It was good experience and I benefited from being included in the team. Living in Woodford, I was never further than an hour's drive from competitions. This was a big help geographically, as Mother was able to drive me to events, there and back in the day, otherwise I am not sure how she would have managed. The only serious travel I had done, apart from holidays in Suffolk, was going to Huntercombe Golf Club in Oxford, not very far compared with the junior circuit today.

The International Junior Tour in Florida was considered out of reach. The LTA had therefore arranged a training week at Huntercombe in January for promising juniors aged 13 to 15. It had a nine-hole golf course, two indoor tennis courts, two squash courts and accommodation. This new innovation to the LTA training programme was good timing for me as it only took place in 1953 and 1954. Huntercombe was owned by Viscount Nuffield, who, as William Morris, started the famous car company. Accommodation consisted of two dormitories: one for the girls, and one for the boys. There were ten of us. Dan Maskell was in charge, assisted by the professional coach, Fred Paulson. It was a fun and concentrated week of training. If we were not playing on the courts, we were practising against the walls of the squash courts.

But the indoor facility had seen better days and, often, leaves blew in through the draughty doors. On one occasion, an elderly man appeared in an old coat carrying a broom. We stepped out of his way thinking he was the groundsman. He stopped and turned to us.

"How very nice to meet you!" he said. "It's so good to see my courts being used."

It was then we realised it was Lord Nuffield himself.

"I apologise for the leaves," he added, and continued on his way with his broom.

Despite the privilege of being coached by Dan Maskell at Wimbledon, which continued to be what I liked best, Mother became frustrated, trying to find practice partners between these lessons. It was not easy to persuade club members to play points with a 13-year-old girl. In desperation, she suggested that golf might be an alternative, as I could practise on my own. Mother was never someone to disagree with, so I joined a junior squad at Chigwell Golf Club. This was organised by a wonderful lady, Mrs Bell. She ran a junior group and, when introducing me to golf, insisted that all I needed was a driver, sand wedge, putter, and 3-, 5-, 7- and 9-irons. I still play 18 holes, aged 81, hoping for that elusive hole-in-one, but to this day I have never been able to move onto the full range of clubs!

Much as I enjoyed my foray into golf and even had my first kiss in a golf hut at Thorpeness in Suffolk (it was a dare, but not very daring!), I hankered after playing tennis. Mrs Bell accepted that tennis came first and when I reached my first Wimbledon semi-final, she sent me a huge bouquet with a card saying: 'Wish you had a golf club in your hand.'

For family seaside holidays, my parents rented a house in Thorpeness. Neighbours from Loughton recommended it as a place suitable for our large family of eight. When there was still a station, we went by train in 1947 and 1948. These holidays were especially memorable for the friends we made when returning year after year, and the activities available for all ages. Father purchased a season ticket for the Meare, a lake with boats of all types, and a holiday membership for the Thorpeness Country Club.

The club had eight tennis courts, including a court for juniors, and a resident coach, Mr Lowe. He was imported from Queen's Club and coached at Thorpeness for the six-week summer season. Antony Payne, a neighbour, and I, both aged 9, used to play most mornings at 8 o'clock on the junior court. Our matches were always a draw, as either we cheated or we didn't know how to score properly! With the bracing North Sea for swimming, our holidays were complete, though I was still waiting my turn to have lessons with Mr Lowe.

There were family tennis tournaments every week. Even Father took part, but none of us wanted to partner him because he volleyed all the balls that were going out! This made it hard to win. He didn't mind, but we did. There was bingo, treasure hunts, a general knowledge quiz and dances on Wednesday and Saturday evenings. I can still remember dancing the Dashing White Sergeant, my favourite, the Gay Gordons and the Paul Jones. I mostly danced with Father. We did not get very far, he only knew one step – and we juniors had to leave at 10pm.

The Thorpeness church had a short service at 10am for half an hour, so we rarely missed an activity. My favourite sermon, by the Rev. Charles Cowley, was about a boy who wrote all his Christmas thank you letters before Christmas. 'Dear Aunty Jane. Thank you so much for your lovely present. It was just what I wanted. Love from Neil.' 'Dear Uncle Frank. Thank you so much for your lovely present. It was just what I wanted. Love from Neil.'

Neil wrote 10 of these thank you letters but left them at school by mistake. When he phoned the school, the headmaster told him not to worry, he had found his letters and posted them. A gentle introduction to 'Your sins will find you out!'

All the family entered the nearby Framlingham Tennis Tournament. I was finally included, aged 11. It is the second oldest tournament in the country with 47 events. There was something for everyone and, most importantly, a marquee with home-made cakes! Errors in administration were not uncommon. Once, in a junior event, I played a gruelling two-hour match against an opponent in the morning, which I won. Only to find I had played the wrong person. Then I had to play the correct opponent in the afternoon. Fortunately I won again! Win or lose, it was expected that competitors would volunteer to umpire, and a victory meant buying your opponent a drink, usually squash, after the match. Holidays at Thorpeness introduced me to the Suffolk tennis scene which was a step up the ladder for me, and a route to senior competitions without travelling miles.

Framlingham is still a successful grass court tournament. It is a reminder of what sport is about. Not everyone wants to win Wimbledon, and tournaments like Framlingham give people of all ages without ranking points a chance to compete. It encourages a feel-good factor, rather than appearing to be a sport that is difficult to participate in.

Aged 12, I added other Suffolk tournaments to my summer schedule. I played at Felixstowe, Bury St Edmunds, Frinton, and on one occasion I went further afield to Broxbourne in Hertfordshire. Mother took me and sometimes I stayed with local club members who were friends. No one starts by playing at Queen's, Eastbourne and Wimbledon. The climb to the top is a gradual process. These events were the backbone of British tennis, offering vital stepping stones to a higher level. Currently, Italy has proved the importance of domestic tournaments as being the vital ingredient for making it possible to have 10 players now in the top 100. Matteo Berrettini, a Wimbledon finalist in 2021, will surely have many followers and a queue of fans, including me. It is good news to hear that the LTA is increasing its British tournament schedule in 2022.

After our active holiday, I returned home feeling prepared for the Junior Championships of Great Britain, to be held on the red shale court at

Wimbledon in September 1955. I was 14 years old, and already playing senior tournaments, but the Junior Championships of Great Britain was my immediate goal.

There was a transistor radio in our local music shop. It was hideous: blue and grey with a chrome top, but I loved it. My parents promised that if I won Junior Wimbledon, I could have the radio as a prize. Another piece of good news was that I had stopped growing in height. Physically, much else was happening, although puberty was not a word I ever heard at home. I only learned about grown-up things from friends at school. That's what we discussed during break-times between lessons, not work-related topics.

Despite being the youngest in the draw at Junior Wimbledon, surprisingly I reached the semi-finals. My opponent was Ann Haydon, the defending Champion. Later, as Ann Jones, she became Wimbledon Champion in 1969. The match took two and a half hours, and I lost 7-5 in the third set. It was a humdinger of a battle and spectators congratulated me on such a close semi-final. I thought maybe I had done enough to earn the transistor radio. After all, I was only 14, and Ann was 16 and it was an U18 event. But no. I had to wait. Mother said the transistor radio was only for winning. I was bitterly disappointed, but Mother never gave way.

At this stage of my development, Slazenger, agreed to supply me with two tennis rackets a year, and Dunlop gave me two pairs of Green Flash shoes. These were canvas, with a herringbone pattern on the soles to prevent slipping.

Ted Tinling, the famous dress designer, invited me to wear his handmade tennis dresses. This was a thrill after Mother's home-made kit. Ted Tinling was a larger-than-life character who only designed outfits for the top tennis players. His dresses were beautifully tailored and much sought-after. Many great players were dressed by Ted, but it proved to be the last time I would wear Mother's home-made designs.

Not to be ungrateful, I had grown out of my pillow slips, and although she upgraded me to her new design of square-necked dresses, with the skirt a little too long, we were both delighted to move on. While this was sponsorship of a sort, no money was exchanged. It was unusual for someone so young to have their equipment taken care of and I felt grown-up to have arrived at this point.

Sterling Henry Nahum, known professionally as Baron, invited me to a photo shoot at his smart London studios

In play at Roehampton Club, 1956

GOLF CLUB HOUSE, HUNTERCOMBE.

Huntercombe House, then owned by Lord Nuffield, was the venue for the LTA's training programme for the top juniors, with head coach Dan Maskell, in January 1953 and 1954. Huntercombe had two indoor tennis courts

Being coached by Dan Maskell at The Queen's Club

Clockwise, from above:
**Representing Essex. At
Thorpeness County Club
with coach Ernest Lowe
in 1956. Winning the
Junior Championships
of Great Britain, age 15**

Chapter Six

THE UNEXPECTED

The following year in 1956, aged 15, I started to win senior tournaments and had victories at Cumberland, Connaught, Roehampton and Hurlingham. These were all part of the British hardcourt season in April and May. I was still, however, too young to play at Wimbledon due to the age limit of 16. Instead, the LTA selected me for two senior international matches. To be included in senior matches was what I had been hoping for!

The first match was in June on the grass courts at Surbiton Tennis Club in Surrey. I beat Béatrice de Chambure, the French No.4, which justified my selection. It was an exciting entry into the senior international scene.

My second match, in July, took place far from my familiar surroundings. I travelled by train to Scotland with a team of two men and two women. Our captain was Robin Kipping, a British International. We stayed at The Royal Hotel in Edinburgh, which was all very formal. Up until then I had never been further than Oxford. Edinburgh was an undertaking that was overwhelming, and I felt out of my comfort zone after the long train journey. At 15, in a senior team, I did not want to let the side down. The match was played at the Craiglockhart Tennis Centre. This had a large stadium surrounding a lush grass court. I beat the Scottish No.1, Heather McFarlane, and also won the Scottish Championships, which further cemented my reputation in the senior game. The team were supportive, Edinburgh was not daunting at all and we were delighted to have a win.

In September 1956, after my international debut, at last I did win the British Junior Championships at The All England Club. Receiving a letter of congratulations from Dorothy Round Little, a former Wimbledon Champion, was the icing on the cake. She believed I could win Wimbledon. The final was against Ann Haydon, the defending Champion, and was a repeat of our 1955 semi-final. Once again it was another two hour, three-set battle with my transistor radio still in the shop window at the Woodford Broadway music shop. It was not an easy match, but having lost the first set, I managed to win: 1-6, 8-6, 6-4. I was sent two quotes after winning. One likened me to Herbert Sutcliffe the cricketer: 'Christine can be beaten time and time again without allowing the fact to depress her.' And the other: 'Christine has an obvious genius for the game and a match-playing temperament that burns like a flame in moments of stress.' I was proud to read those comments, although I did not know Herbert Sutcliffe. After this win, I finally did hold the transistor radio in my hands. It was clearly not a popular item after a year in the shop window, but it meant everything to me, and I have kept it as a memento.

At 15, my junior career was virtually over. I was taller than all the juniors and most of the seniors. How I hated that, and I still shed tears and grumbled to my parents that it was unfair and their fault. Looking back, I can see that my height was an asset and it helped me make that difficult transition from junior to senior tennis. But when people told me it must be wonderful to reach all those high volleys and overhead smashes, I wanted to say: 'Yes, that is true, but I am not on a tennis court all the time.'

When tournament success and practice took up more and more of my time, I started to struggle with schoolwork. Homework was unfinished and

I could not keep up. At 15, the official school leaving age in 1956, my parents decided I should have a home tutor for my O-levels in 1957. I was sad to leave Braeside, and Miss Wakefield was sad to see me go. She even suggested I could always come back for netball matches. My tutor, Mrs Shaw, lived locally, so distance was not a problem. But she could not match the challenge of Wimbledon. Reaching the semi-finals at 16 meant O-levels would have to wait. Talent cannot be put on hold or kept in a trinket box to bring out later. I suspect my spirit would have been broken had I been held back. Having success early meant that doubts never clouded my outlook. Without success, I can see there could be a tendency to drift and for uncertainties to creep in. This is often the downfall of aspiring youngsters at this difficult stage of transition. Luckily for Emma Raducanu and me, we leapfrogged this predicament and avoided doubting our careers in tennis. Emma, at 18, incredibly combined two A-levels to add to her success. Anything is possible.

Today, choosing sport over education is a dilemma that is a constant challenge. Success in sport cannot be guaranteed. The prospect of having nothing to fall back on is a problem. Our education system leaves little chance of navigating what it takes to be a top sportsperson. In those important years, from 14 to 18, the demands of sport clash with important exams. There are many countries which do not have this pressure. On the contrary, if the child has talent, the whole family gets behind their progress, as it is often the only way for a passport to a better life. Maria Sharapova left Russia aged six with her father, leaving her mother at home, to train at the Nick Bollettieri Academy in Florida. She won Wimbledon at 17 and also achieved financial success through her good looks, with endorsements both on and off the court. Unfortunately, her progress was marred by injury and a drug-related ban. Part of me admires the guts the Sharapovas showed to give tennis a go, but a bigger part of me has doubts about agreeing with such a decision. There are some things in life you cannot put a value on.

Being a parent has made me aware of the treadmill of GCSEs, A-levels, followed by a university degree with the hope of a job. This route is now a financial consideration with no guarantees. Do talent and flair suffer along the way? Probably. Would Beatrix Potter have been able to develop her talent at school today? Education is a different and challenging journey for schoolchildren currently. Professions in the 1950s and 1960s did not rely on degrees, and the majority of jobs lasted a lifetime. Is there a fortune-teller brave enough to predict the future in these unpredictable times? Being an optimist, I believe there will be answers. Surely, Alan Turing, Francis Crick and Alexander Fleming, to name a few, cannot be the only geniuses to make new discoveries and solutions. The Covid vaccine is an example. There must be someone's child or grandchild somewhere with the same talent. I digress from tennis, but education raises questions that parents of talented youngsters want to discuss.

Many years later, at one of my own children's interviews, the headmistress of a prospective school brought up the topic of my own school life. When I explained that I had left school at 15, and tennis had dominated my education, she observed: "We can never fill in all the gaps, can we?" On reflection, her reply reassured me. I felt she had grasped this aspect of my life, with an economy of words that said so much. We can never do it all.

Aged 15, I was eagerly awaiting the winter training programme. The LTA had appointed a new Australian coach, the former Davis Cup player, George Worthington. He took over from Dan Maskell, who became the LTA training manager. I was excited about this next stage. I had played two internationals, won senior tournaments, and was also GB Junior Champion. This made me confident about the opportunity of positive practice ahead. All I wanted to do was get better – and I thought that the LTA training would help to make that happen.

But nothing happens as you expect. When my training programme arrived by post, I read that the new regime was based on squad training. Gone was Dan Maskell's one-to-one focus. My heart sank. I was bitterly disappointed. I started the new programme, but I could see that I was stagnating and began to feel flat. It was an anti-climax compared with the way I had trained in the past. Gone was the input of a one-to-one coach. Hitting in a squad needed to be combined with working on improving my game. Why would I want to change a winning formula? My sights were set on getting better. I was fond of my fellow squad members – we are still friends today, but I had played and beaten them in competitions. I knew it was not a race and that I was the youngest squad member, but this did not lessen my exasperation at standing still. After such a successful year, it was a disappointment. Even Mother had no answer or possible alternative to my training.

Wimbledon was an outdoor venue, and once the winter settled in, we changed to Queen's Club and its indoor courts. It took me an hour to cross London to Queen's Club by Tube; from Woodford Green, I changed at Holborn onto the Piccadilly Line, and there, as always, I got in the last carriage for Barons Court. Strangely, it is the same today as it was then, a narrow station with no lift. The rear carriage aligned with the stairs, and still does, 65 years later. The Royal Ballet School in those days was near Barons Court and I often shared the carriage with ballet students. Once out, they turned left, and I turned right. On one occasion, I spoke to one of the pupils. She was anxious because she was going to have her feet measured to see if she could continue at the Ballet School. That she could be turned away for something outside her control left an impression. I was glad that, with my size eight feet, I was playing tennis. Altogether, it was a two-hour round trip. Until then I hadn't even noticed the journey because I always looked forward to practising with Dan Maskell. By contrast, now the journey dragged and hardly seemed worthwhile.

What had changed was the method of training. I quickly realised I had little to learn from squad sessions, as up until now I had been so used to individual training and the intensity of one-to-one coaching which had taken me to the top of junior tennis and into the senior game.

This selfish streak that I needed as an individual was not a trait to be proud of, but my energies and direction needed to be channelled and encouraged. I did not know how to deal with this unexpected let-down. There were no obvious answers or choices. The bottom had fallen out of my world.

Yet a coincidence I could not have foreseen changed my game, forever. Despite everything, the LTA training at Queen's was fortuitous. Norman Kitovitz was not a member of Wimbledon, but he was a member of The Queen's Club. If the LTA training scheme had not been at Queen's, our paths would not have crossed.

Victory over Béatrice de Chambure, the French No.4, in 1956,
justified my inclusion in senior tennis tournaments

Freshening up before the final at Roehampton, 1957

Chapter Seven

NORMAN

Norman Kitovitz was blunt, funny, intense, controlling and clever. I was nearly 16 when a practice session introduced me to his drive and aspirations. His traits and enthusiasm matched mine. Unknown to me, in the winter of 1956-57, we were on a collision course.

The first communication I ever had from Norman was a telegram when I was 15, wishing me luck in the final of the British Junior Championships at Wimbledon, against Ann Haydon. The telegram read: 'Look at the ball. Play your own game. Forget about Ann Haydon. Fight hard and you will do it. Norman Kitovitz.' Those words, I would learn, were a recurring theme in his strategy.

After winning Junior Wimbledon, I received many telegrams and letters of congratulations, as I mentioned earlier, including a letter from Dorothy Little who, as Dorothy Round, was the last British lady to win Wimbledon in 1937. I was thrilled and flattered that an ex-Champion took the trouble to write to me, so I did not take particular notice of Norman's telegram. I did not know him, nor did I notice he had been following my progress closely. Unexpectedly, and improbably, it was Norman who helped me achieve my ambitions. Being a member of The Queen's Club, he saw that when I practised with the LTA squad, it was not helping me at all. When we met, we chatted as members do, but I was only aware of Norman as a keen tennis enthusiast and a popular member of the club.

He was a good player, who had played at Wimbledon three times. Only once did he win a round, when he beat Tim Henman's grandfather, Henry Billington, in five sets. Norman was charismatic with strong views. Born in Singapore, of Romanian and Jewish ancestry, he attended school in Switzerland before studying Law at Oxford University. He became a member of the Oxford tennis team. Married, with three children, he had a private income and still found time to play many of the British tournaments with considerable success.

It must have been obvious I was unhappy and confused. Leaving Dan Maskell was a wrench. I was certain it was no one's intention to hold me back, maybe being so young, it was felt I could wait in the wings for a bit. But the change of guidelines left me disillusioned. My parents certainly knew I was sad but had no idea what to do, until the day Norman phoned Mother.

They discussed the situation at length and, out of the blue, Norman volunteered to help me himself. He was not a coach; he was more than that. He was a professor of tennis. We arranged a trial session. I had not been on court with Norman before. I was hooked, and six years later he was still my coach. Despite the thousands of hours he dedicated to helping me, Norman refused payment. Money was never discussed. He was also adamant that I never mentioned his name, nor how he helped my career. He never wanted recognition. Curiously, I feel awkward revealing his name, even now, but I have spoken at length with his daughter, Kathy Blake. She had no idea her father had been instrumental in my success. However, she was delighted for her father to be recognised as a crucial part in my career.

Norman's genius was in his ability to impose his thoughts and philosophy on both my game and my mental approach. I, in turn, trusted his belief in my potential. 'Anything is possible. Miracles take a little longer.' This was one of his favourite quotes. He often carried the autobiography of Oscar Wilde, and sometimes a book by Bertrand Russell. In this collision of two very driven people, a hidden spark of rebellion was revealed. Norman had felt excluded from British Team selections because of his foreign name, but that never bothered me. For my part I felt lost after what became a rift over my training schedule with the LTA. Together we shared an intensity that was built on mutual trust. Norman believed I could be No.1 in the world and he knew I trusted in his belief, and that it was my ambition too. However unlikely and improbable this combination was, it worked.

Having taken me on at 16, Norman found my game was basically already formed. I had a big forehand which was dangerous and also my best shot; a slice backhand which, though effective, Norman saw as a weakness; but I had a powerful serve with a 'cracking overhead'; and I liked to volley. My long reach was an asset for my attacking game. Norman did not make any technical changes, but enhanced what I had with hours of practice. He was a much stronger player than me. I never did beat him, but working with him was exhilarating and never boring. He disguised his hard work with humour. His enthusiasm and energy were infectious. His work ethic was inspiring. He especially wanted me to enjoy what I was doing, otherwise he felt my progress would be stunted.

Movement was important. One example was to imagine waiting for a bus that came too close. There would not be time to step back with the right foot and then the left. Instinctively, I would jump out of the way. That was how he wanted me to be on the tennis court, instinctive, but this took hours of practice.

Norman believed British tennis was static, and players should not be standing still to hit the ball. His speciality was the return of serve. I could not count how many balls he must have served to me. Thousands and thousands. Whenever he threw the ball up to serve, he shouted: "And now!" which meant I had to start my preparation as the ball left his racket. It would be racket back, and footwork ready to move in to take the return early on the second serve. Norman stressed timing was vital. Pace was as dangerous as power. His accent on movement went hand-in-hand with his advice on tennis and on life. "Christine, wait, and you wait for ever." His other gem was: "Don't think, just do." So little, says so much. I was enveloped in the Norman bubble and it was intense. I liked it that way. Being so driven I can see there was a chance of my becoming blinkered and even obsessed by my ambition to be the best. Coming from a large family gave me a balance of normality, or as Father would say: "Whatever normal is." This was important to help me cope with success at a young age.

Part of Norman's driven personality was his need for control. He hated seeing me talk to someone who he thought might distract me from his beliefs. I would immediately receive a letter to say he would never go on court with me again. It never happened, of course, but it was upsetting as I relied on Norman, one hundred percent. I needed to be in his control and control he did. He did not coach anyone else.

Norman was not an ordinary coach, but a fanatic. And so was I. This suited my drive to be the best that I could be. To be a champion, to go beyond the ordinary, I had to ceaselessly try harder and harder. Norman made sure this was never a chore. The practice court was where I wanted to be. His energy was addictive and his enthusiasm persuasive.

Norman never travelled abroad, and he only watched if I was playing in London, but I have all his correspondence. He wrote me a letter a week for five years, all tennis-related, with reminders of what I should be doing and thinking. He also wrote a small book of instruction for me to read when I was travelling. His advice was usually best not to be thinking at all. He said: "If you think, it will be fatal." To this day, I realise he was right, and it is still a flaw of mine. When I think of possible ifs and buts, it is never helpful. Not thinking sounds alarming, but it was on the understanding that his quotations on life and on tennis would be second nature. I should not need to waste energy recalling what to do, just play the ball. It was always: 'Play the ball, play the ball, not opponents.' 'We are all creatures of God.' 'Rome was not built in a day, but it was knocked down overnight.' 'Two men looked out from prison bars, one saw the mud, the other saw stars.' His quotes fitted neatly with the many situations I encountered in various tennis scenarios.

The influence of Norman soon came through in my results. His belief that I could be World No. 1 never wavered. At 18, I did become World No. 2. But this was not good enough for him. I had to try harder. This was only doable with Norman. It is not possible to have a coach without a good rapport. I thought the world of him, and he likewise respected the efforts I made to reach my goals. His appearance in my life was fate, coincidence, magic. Who can say? I still believe in fairies at the bottom of my garden. Credit is long overdue for someone who made my career happen. Through him, as Frank Sinatra sang: "For once I can touch what my heart used to dream of."

At 16, coached by Norman, I had reached the Wimbledon semi-finals. The youngest since Lottie Dod in 1887. As a Brit, this record still stands today, 135 years later.

Thanks to Norman, my tennis was lifted out of the ranks of being a potential top player, to arriving at my first Wimbledon, believing, like Norman, that I could win the title. This is what I had imagined from my first memories as a girl aged 10.

My coach Norman Kitovitz with an unceasing stream of telegrams, letters, advice and encouragement from him

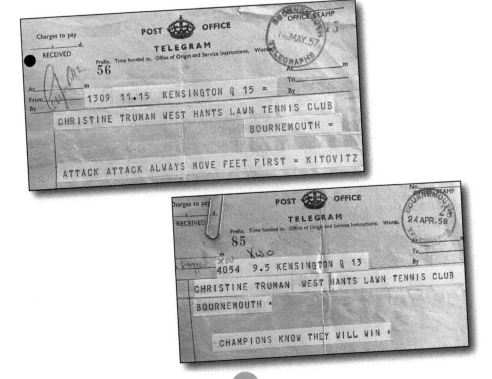

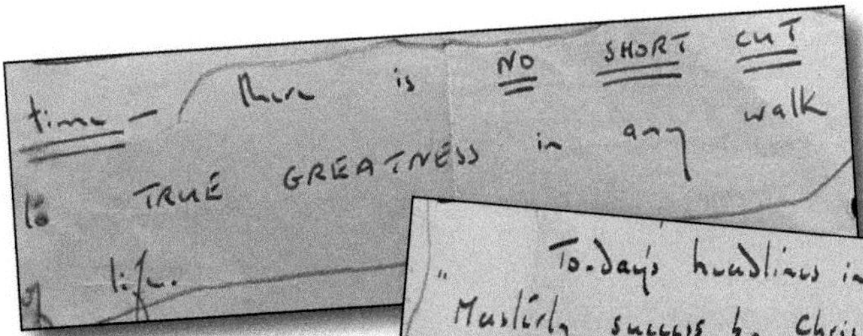

time — / there is NO SHORT CUT
to TRUE GREATNESS in any walk
of life.

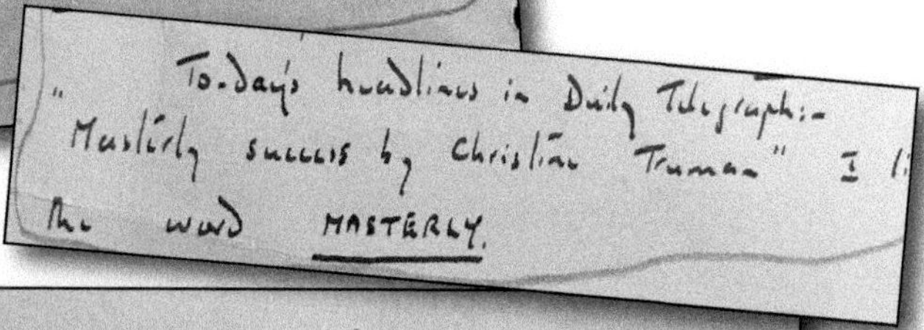

" To-day's headlines in Daily Telegraphic-
Masterly success by Christine Truman " I li
the word MASTERLY.

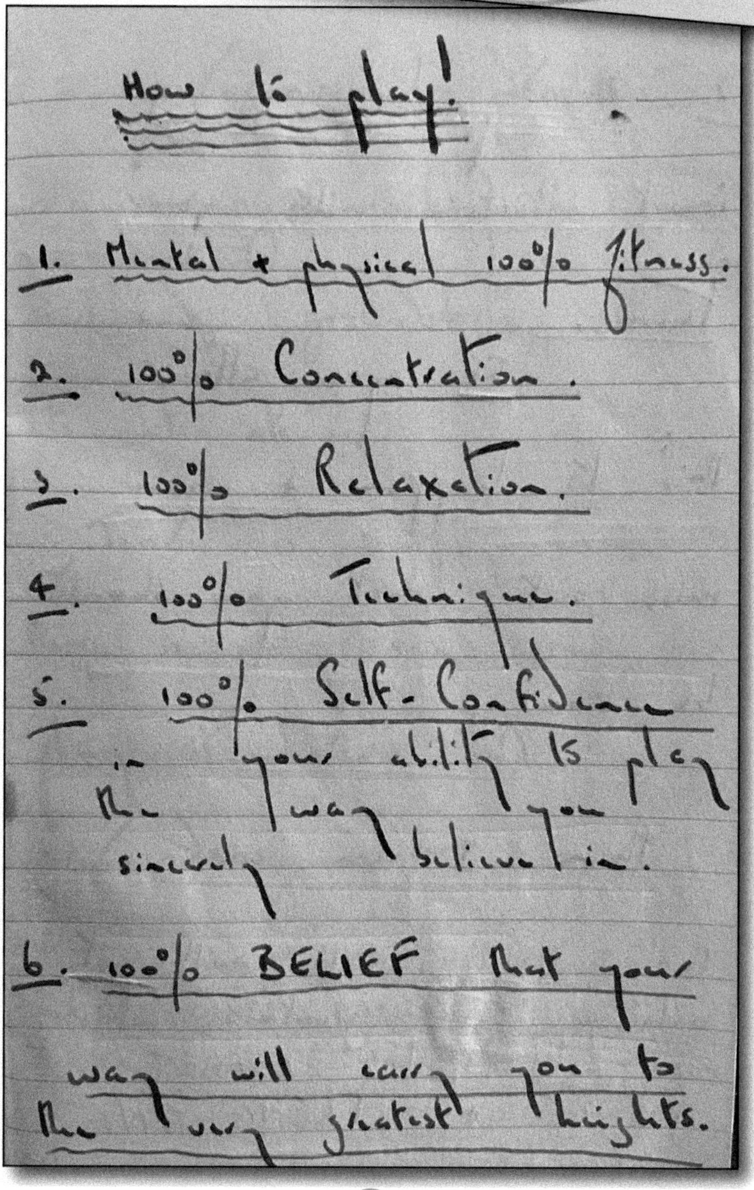

How to play!

1. Mental + physical 100% fitness.

2. 100% Concentration.

3. 100% Relaxation.

4. 100% Technique.

5. 100% Self-Confidence
in your ability to play
the way you play
sincerely believe in.

6. 100% BELIEF that your
way will carry you to
the very greatest heights.

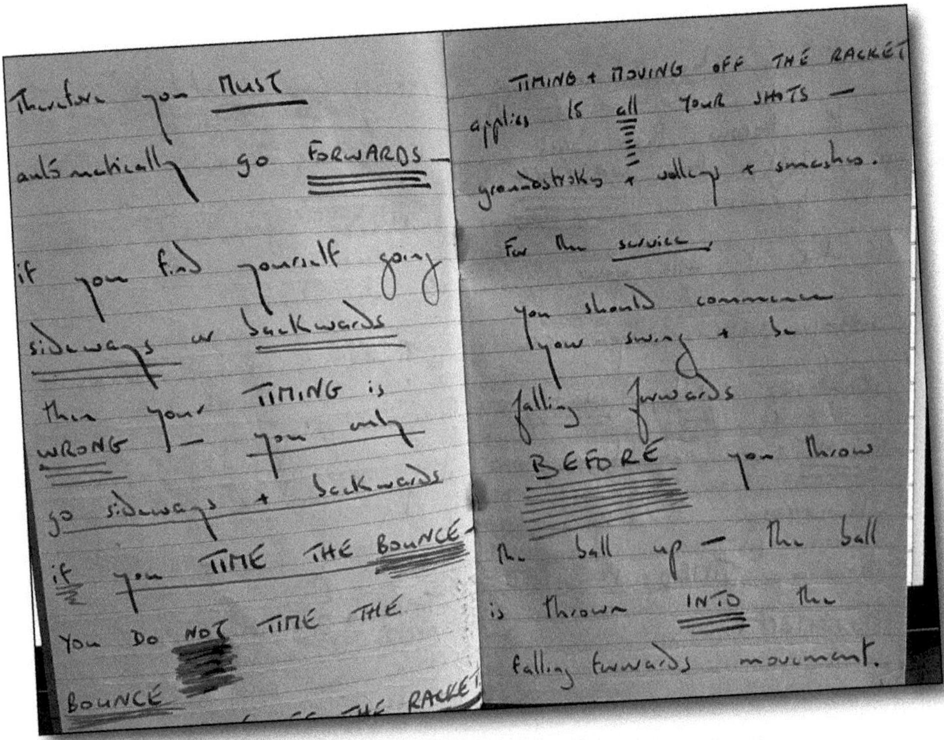

Therefore you MUST automatically go FORWARDS —

if you find yourself going sideways or backwards then your TIMING is WRONG — you only go sideways + backwards if you TIME THE BOUNCE — you DO NOT TIME THE BOUNCE ... off THE RACKET

TIMING + MOVING OFF THE RACKET applies to all your shots — groundstrokes + volleys + smashes.

For the service,

you should commence your swing + be falling forwards BEFORE you throw the ball up — the ball is thrown INTO the falling forwards movement.

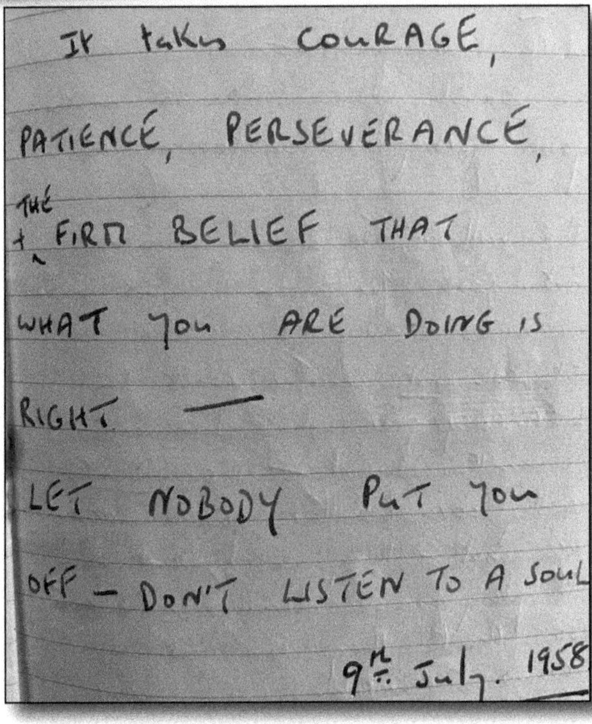

It takes COURAGE, PATIENCE, PERSEVERANCE, + FIRM BELIEF THAT THE WHAT YOU ARE DOING IS RIGHT —

LET NOBODY PUT YOU OFF — DON'T LISTEN TO A SOUL

9th July. 1958

to yourself " Well, I beat her in the Wightman Cup last year, so I must not lose now" — then you were thinking WRONGLY! You do NOT THINK at all about anything! I have told you this 1000000000000 times!!

Listen Christine, your first objective is WINBLEDON — these tournaments before Wimbledon are SIMPLY PRACTICE SESSIONS where you must try your very very hardest to play CORRECTLY ALL THE TIME, so that CORRECTLY BECOMES A HABIT. ...ected immediately

You MUST NOT GIVE UP NOW.

You HAVE ONLY JUST BEGUN TO FEEL + HEAR REAL TENNIS.

I am just as disappointed as you are — but we must all lose sometimes, before we become great champions— AND YOU WILL BECOME GREAT IF YOU CARRY ON PLAYING PROPERLY!!

I heard you won the first set 6-3; why did you not keep up the pressure + win the second set 6-4?

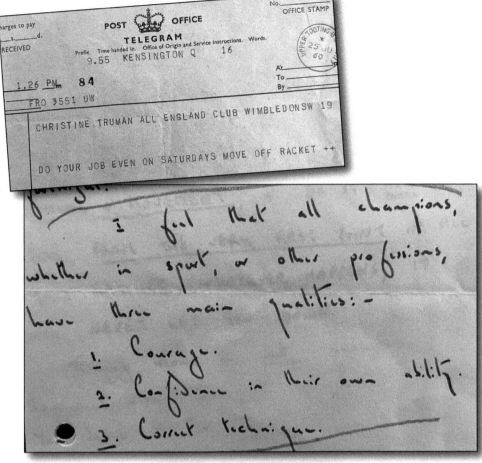

POST OFFICE TELEGRAM

No.
OFFICE STAMP

harges to pay
s. d.
RECEIVED

Prefix. Time handed in. Office of Origin and Service Instructions. Words.
9.55 KENSINGTON Q 16

1.26 PM 84

At
To
By

FRO 3551 UW

CHRISTINE TRUMAN ALL ENGLAND CLUB WIMBLEDON SW 19

DO YOUR JOB EVEN ON SATURDAYS MOVE OFF RACKET ++

I feel that all champions, whether in sport, or other professions, have three main qualities:—

1. Courage.
2. Confidence in their own ability.
3. Correct technique.

Norman would have been proud of this shot

Chapter Eight

WIMBLEDON QUARTER-FINAL

A breakthrough! It was thrilling to reach the quarter-final of my first Wimbledon at 16. This was the first signal of the impact my youth would have on the tennis scene. The press were full of reports of my surprise win in the previous round against Shirley Bloomer, the British No. 1. "Christine looks a Champion," said former Wimbledon Champion, Dorothy Round, in *The Sunday Express*. "Her forehand is a dream." Yet, I apparently played tennis "with something of the savagery of 'Little Mo'" – the nickname for the former US No. 1, Maureen Connolly – who at 19, won four Grand Slam titles in 1953. The ultimate compliment. *The Sunday Pictorial* added: "Hats off for an English 'Little Mo'". Parallels with my heroine were welcome.

My parents were pleased, although they did not show their feelings. It was not their way, but I knew they were proud of me. Father left for the City at 7:30am, as usual. He never took time off work unless I was playing in the final on a Saturday He stuck rigidly to his word. By contrast, Mother phoned all her friends to tell them the news. If it were today, I would be sending texts on my iPhone, but sharing such news instantly was impossible in 1957.

A practice court had been booked for 11 o'clock at Wimbledon. My hitting partner would depend on player availability. Tennis coaches could only spectate, and traditionally, Centre Court and Court One were never used for practice. These stadium courts stood aloof, untouched, waiting for the matches to begin.

At 9:15am I left the house, with Mother driving. We travelled in silence from Woodford Green to The All England Club, a journey of an hour and a quarter by car. I was not nervous; silence was my idiosyncrasy; I needed that quiet space to prepare my thoughts ahead of the match – and conversation was a distraction. In my mind I was rehearsing how I would play and this mental mindset was crucial. Norman believed I could win Wimbledon this year and although this might seem outrageous, his belief simmered in my mind too. Reaching the second week of the Championships, I was a step closer. It seemed possible. Being a driven person, I had always aimed for the top. I recalled Dan Maskell, the LTA coach, taking me, aged 14, onto Centre Court and saying: "Christine, I want you to feel this grass beneath your feet because one day you will play here." Now that day was here, and his words rang in my ears. Was it fate that Dan Maskell was the BBC commentator for my match? Did he remember his prediction? At 16, my ambition knew no limits.

During the Championships the ladies' dressing rooms were graded one, two and three. Dressing Room 3 was in the basement. It was for the unseeded players, the foreign players and the qualifiers. Being unseeded, I was in the basement, Dressing Room 3. We called ourselves 'The Outsiders.' This separation led to dressing room rivalry and it was a great victory for Dressing Room 3 if we had a win over Dressing Rooms 1 or 2.

When I arrived for my quarter-final match, I was greeted with hundreds of letters, telegrams and flowers from fans and well-wishers. For an ordinary girl, unused to this level of attention, it was overwhelming. I could not believe how many people took the trouble to write – fans who did not know me, as well as friends who did. There was no time to dwell on them. I had to get ready.

I opened my hard-back tennis suitcase, my pride and joy, a Christmas present from my parents. The era of soft-sided bags with zips had yet to arrive. The case was distinctive: the outside was beige, the inside maroon. I liked that. There was room for two wooden rackets, a pair of Green Flash shoes with clean laces, white socks, my outfit, a hand towel and toiletries.

It was a hot day. I can't remember who I hit with, but the practice session was good and my timing in tune. This mattered, as I needed to be comfortable with how I was striking the ball until my gut instinct told me I could do no more. I felt confident. I was ready.

There was no players' box in 1957 on the Centre Court as there is now, so after a light lunch in the competitors' restaurant, I collected my guest passes from the Club office. These were Centre Court seats in the stands for my family and Norman.

The clock ticked away. I could see 1:50pm was getting closer. Norman sent me a brief message: "Play the Ball!" I felt strangely removed from everything around me as I changed into my lucky dress and new cardie. Lastly, I made sure my socks and shoes were comfortable, a small but important detail. At 1:55pm, the referee, Colonel Legg, called Dressing Room 3 and requested Miss Truman report to the Centre Court waiting room. Today this formality would sound quaint. The waiting room was a small, basic space behind the Centre Court entrance. It had a few chairs and a picture of the President of The All England Lawn Tennis Club, Princess Marina, hanging on the wall. A steward escorted me. Holding my two rackets, towel and handbag, I was on my own. This was it. I was going to play on the Centre Court at Wimbledon. Dreams do come true.

My quarter-final opponent, Betty Pratt, was already there; Dressing Room 1 being closer to the Centre Court, and she greeted me with a warm smile. At 32, Betty was twice my age, and a member of the US

Wightman Cup Team. Well-wishers told me she was very experienced and had the temperament for big occasions. Comments like this can sow the seeds of doubt, but I knew being here was not a fluke. Norman had drilled me to play the ball, not opponents.

Punctuality is a Wimbledon trademark, and on the dot of 2pm Betty and I walked onto the immaculate grass of the Centre Court. It was bathed in hot sunshine; a perfect day. We turned to curtsey to the Royal Box, an awkward moment in front of 14,000 watching people. It was a bob, not a curtsey. I was more self-conscious about my height than my lack of experience. Although just 16, I was 5' 11¾" and hated being tall. At least I felt confident in my winning Ted Tinling dress. Much to Ted's frustration, I had worn the same dress for every match so far, with my new turquoise cardigan that came from Puddicombes haberdashery store in Woodford Green.

In 1957, there were no players' seats next to the green wooden umpire's chair, just bottles of Robinsons Barley Water, orange or lemon, with a jug of water, for the break at change-of-ends. After I put my two wooden rackets, handbag and a hand towel beside the umpire's chair, the umpire watched whilst I spun my racket onto the grass to see who would serve or receive. Winning the toss, I chose to serve. There was a three-minute warm-up. It felt longer, until finally the umpire called: "Time, please!" There was a hush from the crowd and now, at last, play would begin.

"Miss Truman to serve."

Few moments in my life compare with that day. It was the hottest day at Wimbledon. The papers noted it was 35°C (96°F) in the shade. There were 135 casualties on Centre Court, and 200 cases of fainting. Perhaps it was my reported 'icy coolness,' but luckily, despite being a fair-skinned blonde, I never minded the heat.

The match was a marathon. It could not have been closer and lasted two and a half hours; every point was a struggle. Winning a close first set 9-7, and leading 4-1, in the second set, I had a blip. Betty was quick to come back and win the second set 7-5. At one set all, it looked as though I had blown my chance of victory. Betty was older and wiser, she looked the winner now. But I was oblivious to her experience and did the only thing I knew best and that was to hit out and play my own game. It worked until I led 5-2 in the third set when Betty fought back, producing a flurry of winners, but this time I was ready, and saved my best until last, winning 9-7, 5-7, 6-4. At this moment Betty threw her cap in the air with a smile and said: "Congratulations!" when we shook hands. Matches like that are few and far between and I felt elated to be the winner.

When we walked off the Centre Court, the crowd gave us a standing ovation, as much for Betty as for me, the winner, for although Betty lost the match, her sporting behaviour won her many fans. We became life-long friends.

The press went to town and it seemed the world had paused to celebrate. I was so happy and full of adrenaline I did not want my world to stop. In my first ever press conference I replied to questions: "No, I hadn't been worried about playing on Centre Court. I had looked forward to it." " No, I hadn't expected to get so far in Wimbledon." "A celebration? No, not yet." I had the semi-final on Friday.

On the front page of *The Daily Mirror*, I was: "Giant Killer Christine." And *The Daily Herald* said: "Our 'Little Mo'…the Woodford Whiz Kid."

The News Chronicle made much of the drama of the occasion: "The ice cool girl wins!" In contrast, it was too much for Mother. She collapsed from nervous exhaustion. Millions watched the game on BBC television. It was "almost like some fairy story," said *The Times*.

Arriving home at Woodford Green, photographers were waiting in the front garden. Flashing cameras greeted me. It was an extraordinary moment for an ordinary girl to find the press on her doorstep. They were keen to hear what it was like to play on the Centre Court: "What did Betty say when she lost?" "What was it like to win?" After my Centre Court debut, I could not remember many details, only that I won. The phone never stopped ringing; there was no chance of an early night and my routine was in tatters. Home was chaotic. It was the opposite to all I knew, and I can only say it got worse!

My sister travelled down from Liverpool to stay with us, with her baby boy. In despair I knew this was not an ideal environment when preparing for a Wimbledon semi-final. To be fair, Mother did not think I would still be in the Championships, and family came first. As usual, she said: "Don't make a fuss." I learned that these words were her way of dealing with awkward moments that could not be changed. She stayed up all night in case the baby cried and disturbed me. I doubted Althea Gibson, my semi-final opponent, faced the same predicament. This scenario would have been a comedy sketch, if it were not such an irritating saga. Norman came to my local club at Woodford Green to give me a light practice on my day off before the semi-finals. This saved me a journey into London and was more relaxing as we were able to escape the photographers who seemed determined to get more photographs wherever I went.

Life was changing, but I was yet to realise this, despite being in newspaper headlines, and on TV and radio. Recognition for my achievements was flattering, but the attention was strangely unreal and it was something I would adapt to over time. But for now, I was an ordinary girl who, at 16, had reached the semi-finals at Wimbledon. In 1957, I was the youngest British semi-finalist since Lottie Dod, who won Wimbledon, aged 15, in 1887.

One reporter wrote that Lottie, now aged 85, was following my progress. Sadly, that story proved impossible to follow up. But if she was watching, I

Victory over Betty Pratt to win
the first of my four Wimbledon
quarter-finals, 1957. In those
days there was no sitting
down at change of ends

hope she was impressed. I could not challenge her record, but it was her achievements that gave me the excitement and desire to follow in her footsteps. She was my heroine. My chance lay ahead.

Watching Emma Raducanu in 2021 making her Wimbledon debut as an 18-year-old girl, brought back memories of my own debut at 16 in 1957. Like Emma, I was unseeded with no expectations, but two weeks later everyone knew my name. Despite it being a different era, some things never change. The thrill of seeing a young British girl playing without a care in the world was refreshing. The crowd's support was deafening, but like me, Emma enjoyed the centre stage, and thrived on being our big hope for the future.

Chapter Nine

ALTHEA GIBSON

Forty-eight hours later, at 2pm, I was back on the Centre Court. This time I knew the procedure and had gone through my usual routine of preparations, but I could not escape the atmosphere of excitement and anticipation in the grounds of The All England Lawn Tennis Club. My first Wimbledon semi-final was against the No. 1 seed, Althea Gibson. At 16, my age had caught the imagination of the public, as they could see I was still just a schoolgirl, not long out of sandals and ankle socks. The sports writer, Peter Wilson wrote: "When six-footer Christine lolloped onto Centre Court, it was like a breath of fresh air from the playing fields of St Hilda's." But underneath this image, was a girl who wanted to be a champion and this moment was what I had been waiting for. Being superstitious, I usually stuck with my 'lucky' dress – but Ted Tinling had suggested I wear a new style he had created, with 'Christine' embroidered in red around the waist-line. He persuaded me that today the Centre Court deserved a new look. In hindsight, I should not have listened, although the dress was not the reason I lost!

Before I left Woodford Green with Mother, who was once again driving me to Wimbledon, the photographers were back in the front garden. They wanted a picture of me saying goodbye to my baby nephew, so I posed, clutching the new addition to the family. It was not the photo opportunity

I expected before a Wimbledon semi-final. I just wanted to get in the car and go; my patience was wearing thin, as I did not need this distraction. However, the press intrusion was new to us, and Mother thought it rude to say no.

My practice before the match was erratic, perhaps a tell-tale sign, and the limited court time seemed too short. At 16, I never felt tired, but my determination was being tested. Once again, as an 'Outsider', the walk from Dressing Room 3 to the Centre Court led me through the double doors under the inscription from Rudyard Kipling's poem.

'*If you can meet with Triumph and Disaster*
And treat those two imposters just the same...'

It was to prove a reminder of what being a competitor really meant, as well as a prophecy.

Althea and I met in the Centre Court waiting room five minutes before two o'clock. We had met at Beckenham, a warm-up tournament before Wimbledon, so we knew each other, but no words were spoken as we casually shook hands. I was not nervous. I never went on court thinking I might lose. Norman always quoted: "It is wrong to get used to losing," but I noticed Althea had the poise of a champion, and was an imposing figure.

The match made headlines in the press. Like Betty, Althea at 30, was older and more experienced than me and knew the challenges of the Wimbledon Championships. The front page of *The Daily Mirror* claimed in large print: "Althea will gobble Christine." Norman warned me he would stick this headline round a tennis ball and throw it onto the Centre Court as we made our entrance. My abiding memory of walking onto the grass with Althea Gibson was not the curtsey we made to the Royal Box, but wondering whether Norman would actually throw the ball – and he did! He explained later how he held the ball in both hands behind his head and threw it accurately from the sixth row back in the stands onto the court. I smiled when it landed by my feet and briefly recognised the headline before it was quickly retrieved by a ball boy.

Althea was tall like me. I was not alone after all. She had a big serve with a 'kick', which I found difficult to return. Her game was penetrating and powerful and she had a seriousness of intent which did not falter. A *Daily Telegraph* reporter wrote of Althea: "Gibson, ever pressing netwards, ever on the attack, fighting every point, recoiling only to spring again, played as relentlessly as any woman ever did." Her game was not unlike mine, but on the day she was much better, and I was outplayed. I lost 6-1, 6-1 in a one-sided match. It is not always the case that the loser played badly, but that the winner, Althea, did not allow me to play my game. She dominated the court as though it was her own backyard and dwarfed my efforts with her superior play. She went on to win the Championships, beating the US No.2, Darlene Hard, in the final. It was a historic moment for this popular, sporting competitor when she became the first black girl to win Wimbledon. We became tennis friends in the short time I knew her. In 1958, she turned pro, aged 31. We had attributes in common, such as our height and aggressive game, though I don't think height bothered her at all. I knew she was intrigued by someone of my age, and her words of encouragement were helpful to hear from a champion.

After a standing ovation as we walked off the Centre Court, I felt miserable. Losing was the end of my Wimbledon hopes and any thoughts that I might actually have done well to get this far, aged 16, never occurred to me. In my mind I did not win.

It was a surprise when Princess Marina invited me to have tea in the Royal Box. She sent a message to Dressing Room 3 asking me to join her for a celebration. All those present acted as if there was something to celebrate. But I had lost. I never imagined in my wildest dreams that I would be sitting down to have tea with royalty.

"You look much taller off the court," said Princess Marina, as she greeted me.

These were words I dreaded. I was embarrassed as I seemed to tower over all her guests, and was lost for words. I felt deflated and thought she might have mentioned something about my tennis. Anyway, tea carried on and the honour of that occasion with Princess Marina when we did talk about my first Wimbledon, made my visit to the Royal Box a highlight of my first Championships.

My coach, Norman Kitovitz, who was the reason for my success in reaching the semi-final, wrote to me, saying he kept his promise and threw the ball on to the Centre Court. But why did I not keep mine and play the tennis we had practised? Winning was what mattered. Knowing I had let Norman down made me despondent, although I knew he knew that I had done my best. The intensity of Norman's belief never changed; reaching the semi-final was not good enough. I in turn, thrived on this approach, and wanted to get better.

No one knew that Norman was the reason for my breakthrough. There was to be no recognition. Freddie Trueman sent me a bunch of white roses. He always teasingly emphasised the 'e' in his spelling of the name, 'Trueman'. These compliments and hundreds more from friends and family could not compensate for my disappointment.

Despite all this attention, I did not feel excited at all. The semi-final had given me a taste of what might have been. Getting close was not what Lottie Dod did: she won Wimbledon. Maureen Connolly also won Wimbledon, she did not lose in the semi-final. She wrote me an open letter published in *The Daily Mail*. It was full of heartfelt advice and encouragement. She had been there and knew what to say. She recognised in me: "…the burning desire to win separates the winner from the field…"

She finished with: "Don't brood over that Gibson defeat." She knew I was feeling dejected. Her letter encouraged and inspired me.

Wimbledon, being an occasion in both the national and tennis calendar as the oldest and most prestigious Grand Slam in the world, traditionally ended with a Grand Ball at the Grosvenor House Hotel in London. This was a spectacular finale. I had never been to a ball before, but the Club Committee persuaded me to attend. At 16, 48 hours before the big event, I did not own a formal ball dress. So my older sister, Isabel, came to the rescue and lent me hers. By tradition, after short speeches from the Champions, the band struck up a popular Quickstep and the Men's and Ladies' Champions started the dancing. This added a touch of glamour and I sincerely hoped one day this would be me. My dancing lessons proved useful, with a couple of Quicksteps and a Charleston thrown in during my big night out. It was only when I arrived home after the ball that I realised I had worn Isabel's dress back to front, perhaps not so glamorous that way round! No wonder I did not get to dance with Lew Hoad, the Men's Champion.

This finish to Wimbledon was a mark of the amateur era, when players were obliged to stay for the Ball. Today, only the Wimbledon Champions celebrate their success at the end of the Championships with a Champions' Dinner, while the professional tour moves on, week after week, year after year.

Shortly afterwards, I learned those two imposters, Triumph and Disaster, were inseparable twins. One followed the other. I couldn't match Lottie Dod's record of winning Wimbledon at 15, but I wanted to be the next best. After the disappointment of losing to Althea Gibson in the semi-final, I heard I had been selected for the British Wightman Cup team. This was a famous international women's fixture held annually since 1923, between GB and the USA.

Playing in the Wightman Cup was every British girl's ambition, along with Wimbledon. Although I felt I had earned my place, team selection was not always guaranteed, so I was delighted to be chosen and achieve this honour. It was a chance to represent my country and travel internationally. At 16, I was the youngest member of the team, a life-changing move onto the next step of the ladder.

Losing Wimbledon semi-final to Althea Gibson, 1957

Losing to Althea Gibson in Wimbledon semi-final, aged 16

Leaving home, to play this epic semi-final, with brother Philip sister Elizabeth and baby Kevin

On court with Althea Gibson. But look at the ballboy's long trousers!

Chapter Ten

REPRESENTING MY COUNTRY

Representing my country proved that Father's advice: "Nothing succeeds like success," was true when, after reaching the semi-finals at Wimbledon, I was selected to represent Britain in the Wightman Cup.

I was thrilled to be going to the USA with the team. For me, it was a tour of firsts. It was my first long-haul flight and my first team blazer, a white flannel jacket from DAKS. Playing tennis in the US was my first taste of heat and humidity and my first hotel room with an en-suite bathroom. Above all, it was my first trip without Mother. A 'wow' moment.

We flew from Heathrow courtesy of BOAC, on a plane that had propellers. Seeing propellers going round felt safer to me than flying in a jet today. At least I knew the engines were working. It took 11 hours for our overnight flight, and BOAC gave us a navy-blue zip-up bag for hand luggage. Feeling super-smart, I could say I was now a traveller. I also enjoyed the tray of boiled sweets in cellophane wrappers that the aircrew brought round before take-off and landing. They were supposed to stop the passengers going deaf from the pressure when ascending and descending, but it didn't make much difference, though the sweets were nice.

Arriving in New York for the first time at 16 was astonishing. Everything seemed bigger than London. Tall buildings towered over the city; the Empire State building in those days was the tallest building in the world.

The shops were eye-catching. I bought my first pair of Bermuda shorts in Saks Fifth Avenue. The sweet shops were extraordinary. Some shops just sold fudge. I had never seen that before. Penuche was my favourite. The humidity was draining. I soon learned that too much air-conditioning was the quickest way to catch a cold. But what impressed me most on that first trip to the US was the American approach to life. I found their 'Have a good day!' and 'can-do' confidence uplifting. New York quickly became one of my favourite cities. It has a buzz that should be bottled as a 'must-have' tonic.

Travelling with the team could not have been a better introduction to the tour. I was the youngest member, with Sheila Armstrong, Ann Haydon, Shirley Bloomer, Ann Shilcock and our lovely captain Mary Halford. We got on well and I felt protected as a new girl. There were no money problems. Financially, the trip was paid for, and we had twelve shillings pocket money each week for incidentals. Mother made me some summer dresses for day-wear and put a large box of Persil in my suitcase to remind me to do my washing. For her, my rackets came second to the soap powder. With a tube of shoe-white for my Green Flash canvas shoes and laces, she was satisfied I was properly equipped for the tour.

Throughout my heyday, Mother filed all my correspondence, including every letter I received. But sadly, she did not keep the blue air letters I wrote home when overseas. These were full of my thoughts about the places I visited, with details of my matches. In an age before mobile phones and social media, letter-writing was our only means of communication; even an overseas phone call was expensive and used sparingly. It is a shame, considering all the correspondence that Mother kept, I now have no record of how I felt on my first trip away.

The members of Edgeworth Club near Sewickley, Pittsburgh, were great hosts, and I wore my GB blazer with pride on court. We stayed in a smart hotel where the American actor and pop star, Edd Byrnes, was also staying. He was famous for his duet with Connie Stevens, 'Kookie, Kookie, Lend Me Your Comb'. I felt I had arrived, living with pop stars! We had to get past his barrage of fans wanting a comb each day! The club had a superb swimming pool which I used after the team finished practising. I quite fancied myself as a good swimmer. I don't know why, as I could only do the breaststroke. Because I was easily taken in, Mary Halford called me on an internal phone as a joke and, using a false American voice, she pretended to be the president of the local swimming club and invited me to take part in a swimming gala. Gullible me. I apologised for not accepting, patiently explaining that I was playing in the Wightman Cup match at that time. I did not mention I could only do the breaststroke and was not a swimmer.

On the day of the match there was a grand parade to introduce the teams on court, with both national anthems played to mark the occasion. Margaret duPont, the US captain, was a tennis legend I had only read about. Margaret had won the Wimbledon Championships in singles, doubles, and mixed, and was ranked World No. 1 in 1947. It was intimidating to see her presence on court, knowing how many titles she had won. My Wimbledon reputation as a semi-finalist did not guarantee success on the slow hard courts of the Sewickley club. Hoping for victory in Pittsburgh was perhaps unrealistic against the strength of the US team, and we left, deflated, after a one-sided loss.

Our tour included tournaments on the East Coast and the US National Doubles Championships at the Longwood Cricket Club in Boston. This was held at a separate location from the US National Singles Championships in New York. One of my favourite tournaments was at the Essex County Club in Manchester, Massachusetts. The ECC caters for golf, but has ten grass and ten clay tennis courts, and a full-size swimming pool. Good for practising my breaststroke. The grass courts were immaculate and an excellent opportunity to prepare for New York where the US Nationals were held at the Westside Country Club in Forest Hills.

Owing to my Wimbledon success, I was seeded No.6 for the Nationals by the USLTA. Seeding at this time was less exact than nowadays. Decisions were made by the tournament committee based on a mixture of tournament results and recent successes. This was still the amateur game. There was no computerised ranking process. For the professionals today, it is scrupulously fair, with a rankings system based on computer points gained by wins on the circuit. This was the reason Emma Raducanu had to qualify at the US Open 2021. She had not played enough tournaments to gain a ranking that would have given her direct entry into the main draw. It is history now that she won the title without losing a set. Extraordinary.

For all the excitement and build up, I lost badly in the second round to Lois Felix. This was disheartening. Although Lois had won singles and doubles titles in the US, I lost to someone I should have beaten. I hated being reminded this was all part of the experience of being a top tennis player. For me 'experience' felt like an excuse for losing.

After a tearful phone call home, I was able get a perspective on what had happened, and accepted the tour was a learning curve. After all, these were locations and players I had not encountered before. I agonised over my game. Was Norman wrong to expect so much of me? Or was it me, and my drive to succeed? What did become clear was that together, player and coach, we never accepted defeat. We used it as a tool to practise and get better. I liked that. And it was never a hardship working with someone who had so much belief in my potential. Norman never stopped telling me I could be No.1.

THE LAWN TENNIS ASSOCIATION

Patron: HER MAJESTY THE QUEEN

RIVER PLATE HOUSE · FINSBURY CIRCUS
LONDON, E.C.2.

Telephone: MONARCH 9051 · *Telegrams:* LAWNTENNA, LONDON

3rd July, 1957.

Miss C.C. Truman,
c/o All England Club,
Church Road,
Wimbledon,
S.W.19.

Dear Miss Truman,

You have been selected to represent Great Britain in the Wightman Cup Match v. U.S.A. to be played on Saturday and Sunday, 10th and 11th August, 1957 at the Edgeworth Club, Sewickley, near Pittsburgh.

Arrangements are being made for you to leave London by air on Sunday, 4th August.

Will you please confirm by return that you are able to accept this invitation.

Yours sincerely,

[signature]

Slazengers Limited

LAURENCE POUNTNEY HILL · CANNON STREET · LONDON · E C 4
TELEPHONE: MANSION HOUSE 7755 · TELEGRAMS: SLAZENGER, CANNON, LONDON · CABLES: SLAZENGER, LONDON

Miss C. C. Truman,   CONFIDENTIAL
10, Snakes Lane,
Woodford,
Essex.   26th January, 1956.

Dear Christine,

Just a line to tell you that we have reduced your Special Terms for rackets for this year to purchase tax only. This will also apply to restrings. Therefore, the only charge we will be making will be 25/3d. on each new racket and 8/7d. on each restring. This of course is a government tax and is unavoidable.

We hope that you will have a most successful season and we would like you to know that if there is anything at all we can do to help you at any time, we will always do our best.

Yours sincerely,

[signature]

DCG/JT.

Chapter Eleven

FAME AND FANS

On returning from my first trip to the USA in 1957, I walked straight into controversy. Timing was not in my favour. My new status as an international player created unexpected problems.

I flew in to London from New York on a Monday. The Junior Championships of Great Britain started the next day, Tuesday. Playing so soon was not a welcome prospect. But I was the defending champion, and it was expected by the LTA that I would play my part.

However, this was not without opposition. Some tournament officials thought I should not be allowed to play. I was a Wimbledon semi-finalist, Wightman Cup player and defending champion. Although only 16, it was thought unfair for me to compete with the other juniors as I would be too good. There were more who might have argued that I was getting too big-headed if I withdrew. There could be a statement that I was getting 'ideas above my station'. A 'no-win' situation.

I did play, but achieved a one-sided victory. After this I did not play junior tournaments again. Mother wanted me to play the next year to achieve the triple crown and equal the record of the British player Betty Nuttall – but it was not allowed. I was relieved, as it was an unpleasant atmosphere to take part when feeling unwelcome. As usual, I was taller than all the juniors, which made me feel awkward, as it was thought an unfair advantage. Did no one understand? It was not an advantage I could help. In my eighth decade, I am just getting used to my height.

Having fame and recognition as a successful 16-year-old semi-finalist at Wimbledon was flattering. But inside, I was the same ordinary girl, I felt no different. I still slept in the same bed, ate the same food, wore the same clothes and had the same friends. I did not want to be noticed. I shed many tears for being tall. I did not want to stand out. As a teenager it was normal to want to fit in with the crowd. And yet my life was very different. This realisation that I was 'famous' was strange. Sometimes people think of a household name as not having normal feelings, and of being somehow different, but I had the same emotions and notions as anyone else. Mostly looking for, and hoping to meet a knight in shining armour was a dream, as it was for many young girls. My height added to the insecurities that a 16-year-old suffers, for one reason or another.

In a queue in our local Woodford Green bakers, I was tapped on the shoulder and taken aback to be told by a stranger: "You look taller off the court than on." I suddenly realised I was public property. Being in the papers and the public eye, I was easily recognised, and found it odd that strangers would make personal remarks. Another time in the local chemist's, a lady thought she was being helpful by saying: "Christine, you need to wear more makeup now you're famous." Again, I was flabbergasted that how I looked mattered to someone who did not know me. Of course, fans felt they did know me, be it in the bread queue or at the chemist's. These moments were new to me because I was supposedly famous.

'Sweet sixteen and never been kissed' was not quite true. But at last, it did change. Not a lot, but a bit. Out of the blue, an army cadet phoned my home. He explained he was doing an army intelligence course, which entailed him being dropped in the middle of nowhere with ten shillings and an official letter to say who he was. His instructions were, in no particular order, to produce a stick of rock with his name through; to get an autograph from Field Marshal Montgomery, who was in Paris at the time; and to have his photograph taken with me – all in the space of 48 hours. This unexpected effect of fame produced a touch of romance. He did not get to Paris, but, after a phone call of explanation, the poor chap arrived in Woodford Green on the point of exhaustion, by foot. On a hot day in army uniform, he produced a small Brownie camera. Mother was there, of course, to keep an eye on things. She also had to take our photograph. My cadet and I got on well over his well-earned cup of tea and struck up a sparky conversation. I finally received a letter from him. Tucked into the envelope with our black and white photograph was a short note: an invitation to a date. I now had a boyfriend.

There was no fairy-tale ending. We saw each other whenever possible, when travelling did not get in the way for both of us. The combination of the tennis circuit and army life did not bode well. Three years later, my four-month tennis tour in Australia was a passion killer. Absence no longer made the heart grow fonder. I still have the silver serviette ring with my name engraved in his own handwriting. It marked the end of our special three-year army and tennis-interrupted romance. Heartbroken, I shed tears as our lives went in different directions. Being a famous tennis player did not mean emotions did not exist.

This encounter with fame was not a one-off. The end of 1957 and the beginning of 1958 became an introduction to life as a 'Household Name'. What I didn't expect was the number of invitations I'd receive to so many events: fetes, dances, church bazaars; some of them glamorous, like film premieres. I could not accept most of them because of training. Although I appreciated the recognition of the press for my achievements, fame was different: similar to a cake mix of celebrities without a clue of where I belonged. However, there were two invitations I did accept.

One was to the Savoy Hotel on the 16th January, my birthday. This was an invitation to a sporting lunch, hosted by the Variety Club of Great Britain, where I was promised a big surprise. I could not believe it when the staff of the Savoy Hotel unveiled an enormous birthday cake to celebrate my seventeenth birthday. I blew out the candles with the help of cricketer Tony Greig, gold-medal swimmer Judy Grinham, and encouraged by Billy Butlin. A heady moment. I was not sure how Billy Butlin's holiday camps were connected with my birthday, but it was a special treat and I felt proud to be worthy of these celebrations.

My other invitation was from Christina Foyle to her Foyle's Literary Luncheon, also at the Savoy. I sat next to a classical musician who asked me about my training schedule. I thought I had impressed him, but no! He told me that Yehudi Menuhin started much younger than I, and spent more time practising his violin each day than I did on the tennis court.

The next day in the post, my Foyle's lunch companion sent me an autobiography of Yehudi Menuhin and his family. Reading of his dedication in his young life made a big impression on me, and I realised that he gave concerts at a much younger age than I was when I competed at Wimbledon. I became a fan, but sadly, we never met. Subsequently, I was invited to present some awards at his music school in Cobham. I had hoped to meet the man himself but, unfortunately, Yehudi could not attend. I'm not sure what the music students thought of receiving their music awards from me, a tennis player!

One other musical connection was two lines in *The Evening Standard* newspaper social diary in 1960. It stated that the cellist Jacqueline du Pré had a 'Christine Truman haircut.' I wonder whether she knew that.

If I compare fame today with my own experience, it is not dissimilar, except I did not have a mobile phone, agent or Facebook, Instagram or Twitter account. For me, the drawback of fame was not modern technology,

A Variety Club of Great Britain lunch at The Savoy happily coincided with my 17th birthday, and here I am with the swimmer Judy Grinham and Billy Butlin

but being recognised when I stepped outside the front door. From the age of 16, I found this was the hardest part of being famous. In 1957 my life changed overnight from being simply a schoolgirl who became a tennis star, after reaching the Wimbledon semi-final. There were headlines: "Christine, tennis sweetheart." "Christine, the darling of Wimbledon." "Christine, the Centre Court heroine." This was fame for my achievements, which was flattering, but although I was not in danger of being mobbed, I did not like being spotted on private occasions. Dining out was not when I needed to sign autographs. Nowadays, people would be asking for selfies as well. Not sure I could have coped with those.

The fact that I had no modern technology was normal. There were no mobiles, Instagrams, iPads or computers in the 1950s. But what I do have are the thousands of letters that Mother kept from my tennis career. Sadly, there were too many to mention them all, but will emails in the future mean the same as holding the printed words in your hand? Can they match the immediate warmth in reading letters from fans such as Johnny Hawksworth, the double bass player with the Ted Heath Band, glowing congratulations from The Dowager Viscountess Ashbrook, or a card from Beryl Ryland, an ex-suffragette prisoner. Either way, the phenomenon of fans who are moved to send a message never fails to amaze me.

Chapter Twelve

PREPARATION

During the winter of 1957/58, I took the chance to improve my training routine. Norman forecast that hard work in the off-season would set me up for the year ahead. No resting on my laurels or slacking; reaching the semi-finals of Wimbledon was not good enough for Norman. We were to practise for the goals ahead. There were a few covered-court competitions, but the bulk of the winter months were spent getting fitter and improving my game.

The US tour had made me realise I needed to work on my fitness, so that winter saw two changes to my routine. First, I met Geoff Dyson, the Amateur Athletic Association coach who lived near Woodford Green. A mutual friend recommended Geoff as someone who could improve my speed and strength around the court. Geoff's wife, Maureen Gardner, was an athlete who won a silver medal for hurdling at the 1948 Olympic Games. Between them, they knew a great deal about fitness. Just talking to Geoff made me feel fitter!

Geoff introduced me to his new drill called 'circuit training'. He learned about circuit training from a team of Cambridge academics who discovered that a set of exercises done at speed kept them fit, without taking more than 10 minutes out of a busy day. Geoff assessed what I needed, and devised six exercises: 20 squat jumps, 10 press-ups, 20 stool steps, 20 squat thrusts, 8 barbell lifts from bent knees and 5 brick-winding exercises to strengthen my wrists. For this, a brick was tied by string to a handle that I had to roll up and down. Needless to say, nowadays, the bricks and string have been replaced by more suitable equipment. You won't find a brick in the gymnasium today. This circuit was to be completed three times against the clock, three days a week.

I took this on and worked hard at it. At first, I struggled to finish and hated these exercises. But with a stopwatch, I could see an improvement. 10 minutes became nine minutes, then eight minutes, then…Geoff never let me cut corners on the exercises and blew a whistle if I cut short the correct number of repetitions. This supervised training made a huge difference to my strength and stamina, and I continued to rely on circuit training in my off-seasons.

Although I was '16 going on 17', like all maturing teenagers I thought I knew more about life than my parents and I felt sorry that they didn't know as much as me. Living at home in Woodford Green gave me a base and a solid background to work from. With the good fortune of Norman's generous coaching, Geoff Dyson's training, and willing hitting partners, there were few overheads. With an off-peak season ticket for the Tube, Father maintained that being a tennis player cost no more than being at school.

On the three mornings I was not doing circuit training, Mother drove me at 8am, with a bucket of tennis balls, to my local club, Woodford Wells. The club had a purpose-built practice wall, where I hit 100 forehands, 100 backhands and 100 volleys, followed by serving a bucket of 25 balls twice, up and down the court. This routine was completed before breakfast. A practice wall is never to be underestimated. I remember watching the Australian Davis Cup team, under the captaincy of Harry Hopman, preparing for the Wimbledon Championships in 1956. They practised volleying up and down the walls of the racquets court at Queen's. It was mesmerizing to watch the speed of their reflexes, even with a wooden racket. Many champions have started playing tennis by hitting balls against a garage door or brick wall.

At 9:30am I went by Tube from Woodford Green to Barons Court station near The Queen's Club, five days a week. The ticket collector at Barons Court got to know my schedule and followed my progress. He kindly sent me a telegram of congratulations after I beat Althea Gibson in the Wightman Cup. Coaching with Norman started at 11am, until lunchtime. I never remember a lesson without his gift of endless energy – and always something that made me smile. His enthusiasm kept me enthralled, and his belief believable. He insisted perfection was not possible, but I still tried hard to see if that was true.

After lunch, a Queen's Club member would challenge me to competitive sets. I preferred practising against men for stronger opposition. This gave me the chance to put into play what I had been practising, a vital exercise for my progress.

My second change happened on the way home when I got off the Tube at Hyde Park Corner. The principal of the Arts Educational College, which was then situated next to Hyde Park Corner station, invited me to join the College for a daily tap and modern dance class. These ran from 4:20pm to 6pm. I still go to tap dancing classes in Suffolk today. All the students had to attend, whatever their speciality. The Head had followed my career and suggested these classes might help my movement and footwork. She told me that C B Fry, the legendary cricketer and greatest all-round sportsman of his time, enjoyed ballroom dancing. Darcey Bussell I was not, but I loved these sessions. They were a complete contrast to the rest of my day, and invigorating. Most of the students warmed up doing the splits. I never quite joined them, but I can still do a shuffle, hop, step, ball change in my tap shoes, and found this precise, controlled exercise very helpful for both my deportment and footwork. Arriving home at 7pm, I was exhausted.

Weekends saw more tennis. Some of the Essex Men's County Team kindly volunteered to practise singles with me at the Connaught Club at Chingford, near home. It was beneficial to hit against their extra strength. The county ladies preferred doubles to singles. My favourite sets were against Francis Wallis, a self-made businessman and once a reserve for the Davis Cup Team. When he was short of time, he arrived by helicopter, landing on the grass courts of the Connaught Club. This made me feel that my practice was a priority in his busy life. We both hated losing and never quite finished our hard-fought matches before he had to fly his helicopter back to work. Tragically, he died flying his own plane back from a tennis match in France. His popularity and love of tennis were a sad loss for the Connaught Club and his friends. Today, the mirror the Wallis family gave as a wedding present hangs above my sitting room fireplace.

My brother, Humphrey, now a member of the Connaught Club, was also a regular hitting partner. At last I was good enough, and his practice undoubtedly helped me to improve. He was a successful doubles player and we played mixed doubles together at Wimbledon for many years. We reached the quarter-finals in 1959. When I was 18, Harry Hopman, the Australian Davis Cup captain, was on tour with his team. He approached Mother to ask if I would play mixed doubles at Wimbledon with his new prodigy, Rod Laver. Mother said: "Certainly not, Christine plays with her brother Humphrey." I did not know that she had turned down Rod Laver. Many years later, at a Wimbledon get-together, Rod Laver said: "Christine, you are the only player to have turned me down."

Occasionally, I would be invited to the Finchley Manor Club to practise with Bobby Wilson, the British Davis Cup player. I suspect Bobby was under pressure from his mother, who encouraged my visits, making a delicious tea for us afterwards. The tennis fraternity teased me as a possible bride for Bobby, but there was never any substance to this rumour. His mother and my mother became firm friends when spectating together during the British hardcourt season. Were they match-making, or watching matches? I will never know. When Bobby Wilson died, not long after my husband in 2020, Elizabeth, his wife, told me that his mother had always hoped he would marry me. We laughed about this and also at the large portrait his mother kept of me on the mantlepiece. Was this a reminder for Bobby? In his mother's later years, when she was getting more confused, we still exchanged Christmas cards. In 1989 I sent her an official Wimbledon Christmas card which had a picture of Boris Becker and Steffi Graf receiving their Champion's trophies. She wrote back saying she was pleased to see my children were doing so well!

The gruelling winter regime of 1958 saw me move up the rankings. My year started by winning four British hardcourt titles, with victories over my great rivals Ann Haydon and Angela Mortimer. In Europe, Shirley Bloomer and I won the Italian Ladies' Doubles title. This was an unexpected triumph, at 17, after I lost in the first round of the Ladies' Singles to Italian No.1, Silvana Lazzarino. Silvana was a tiny dark-haired Italian. Her size disguised her talent for hitting high lobs into the sun, and for slow balls, with no pace, encouraged by the enthusiasm of the Italian crowd, clapping my mistakes. This was new to me. I had to adapt to this style of tennis. Learning to smash consistently helped, not forgetting to ignore the applause and the noise of the spectators.

I soon learned to accept it as usual for the crowd to support their home players and I learned to block out the distractions. It is sometimes seen as additional pressure on local hopefuls who fear letting down their supporters. I am always surprised to hear that the back-up of a crowd can be a worry and that their hopes and expectations, on occasion, can weigh too heavily. This is a pity. When playing international tennis, players are often against the crowd favourite. Roger Federer comes to mind as a role model, who no one wants to see defeated wherever or whenever he is on court.

Throwing my coins in the Trevi Fountain was a must; I grew to love playing in Rome, and if I hear the pop song of 1958, *Volare*, it reminds me fondly of the Foro Italico, the grand stadium where the Italian Championships are still held.

After winning the doubles in Rome, I reached the quarter-final of the French Championships in Paris, which was an improvement on the year before. This encouragement made my hard work worthwhile. Now I looked forward to playing on my favourite surface: grass.

During the winter of 1957/58, I met Geoff Dyson, the Amateur Athletics Association coach, who introduced me to circuit training. Note the brick, barbells and back wall for inspiration

A wonderful telegram to receive, from the ticket collector at Barons Court
Tube station. Below, in conversation with Bobby Wilson, Davis Cup player

Chapter Thirteen

WINNING THE WIGHTMAN CUP

The twenty-ninth Wightman Cup match was the next major event on the tennis calendar. It was to take place a week before the Wimbledon Championships on what is now known as 'The Old Court One', at The All England Club, with the Duchess of Kent in attendance. The United States were predicted to make it their twenty-ninth consecutive win. They were confident, having Wimbledon Champion and the formidable World No.1, Althea Gibson, on their side.

Ann Haydon, Shirley Bloomer, Anne Shilcock, Pat Ward and I represented GB. Mary Halford was our captain again, and we stayed together in a hotel near Wimbledon. To be a team member for a week was a welcome change from life on the circuit as an individual.

The 1958 Wightman Cup proved to be a very special triumph for me. After the official introductions on the first day of play, Shirley Bloomer, Britain's No.1, was drawn to open the proceedings against Althea Gibson, the US No.1. As predicted, it was a one-sided result. Althea looked strong, dominant and confident. She did not allow Shirley a look-in. I did not watch the whole match because I had to prepare to play next; it was important not to get involved emotionally in other matches, but I saw enough to see why Althea was a champion. Her presence was awesome, but I was not daunted and knew I must focus on my game. Playing after

Shirley, as No.2 for GB, I beat the US No.2, Dorothy Knode. She had a baseline game that did not threaten my style, and I won comfortably in two sets. The teams were now level at one match all. Following the singles, Shirley and I pulled off a doubles win against Dorothy Knode and Karol Fageros. Karol was perhaps better known for her gold lamé panties, than her tennis. But her outfit was deceptive because she was a strong competitor and we were relieved to win. GB were now leading 2-1. We were ahead, but not complacent.

Day Two started with a surprise phone call before breakfast from Father. It was unusual for him to make phone calls, rather than Mother, let alone chat. He told me I needed to beat Althea Gibson if we were to win the Wightman Cup. I was surprised by this sudden insight, and thought he was joking. This was so unlike his usual advice: "Don't forget, Christine, nothing succeeds like success." But he meant every word he said.

After a team breakfast, we made our way to the club for a warm-up. I was excited. I knew I had nothing to lose against Althea. She was the Wimbledon Champion. Norman suspected I would play Althea when the teams were announced, so he had served hundreds of balls to me in the past two weeks, imitating her kick serve. His attention to detail never wavered, so I was well prepared.

At 2pm Shirley Bloomer started her match first, against Dorothy Knode – and lost. We were now equal at two matches all. There was a sense of the inevitable when I stepped onto Court One with Althea Gibson. I hated that predictable atmosphere. Nobody thought I had a chance. Except me, Norman and, surprisingly, Father. It took me a while to settle, and Althea was in control when she won the first set 6-3. Persevering with the tennis that I had practised, I knew I was not beaten. Gradually the tide turned, and Althea was startled when I won the second set with fewer mistakes, and attacking the net whenever I had the chance. This was not a flash in the pan, although no doubt Althea thought it was. The third set was touch and go. I said to myself: 'Keep going!' Fist pumps had not yet arrived. Althea forged ahead, and I was 4-2 down. Somehow I found a second wind and pulled back to four games all. Althea now served for a 5-4 lead. Being the Wimbledon Champion, she was still in charge; she looked imposing, as she stood, ready to serve. But my racket felt like a magic wand, an extension of my arm. Everything I touched turned to gold. I broke her serve to lead 5-4, with returns I knew I had played on the practice court but now it was for real – they were winners! Was Althea rattled, I don't know, but it was now me, not Althea, to serve for the match. Changing ends, I was calm. Why? I can't explain. But matches hang on these crucial moments. I knew it was possible to win. Both captains traditionally sat either side of the umpire's chair for advice and support. But Mary Halford knew not to say anything that might break my trance-like concentration. The atmosphere was electric as I served for the match. With no mistakes, nor unforced errors, I won. Never in doubt, I clinched victory 6-4 in the third set. The elation was overwhelming from the packed Court One.

The crowd thundered their applause while Althea just smiled at the recognition of my win. My best memory of beating Althea was her sporting generosity. When we shook hands, there were no excuses, no ice packs, no niggling injuries, just: "Well done, Christine! You were too good for me today." This was refreshing and allowed me to realise that I had played well enough to win against the defending Wimbledon Champion. Now, when I look back at this moment in time, it features as truly one of the highlights of my heyday; Althea was unbeaten, the defending Wimbledon Champion, the US Champion and top seed at Wimbledon – and to win on Court One in front of a home crowd was a moment that I have treasured ever since.

Ann Haydon bravely won the crucial seventh match, and we won the cup by four matches to three. This was our first Wightman Cup win against the US for 29 years. Mary Halford later insisted that I won her an OBE for being captain.

The traditional Wightman Cup dinner was held at the Dorchester Hotel. Althea and I were photographed together, smiling, many times. We were friends, no hard feelings. After a late night, the Wightman Cup teams attended the famous annual Charity Garden Party at the Highgate home of Lady Crossfield. This was a tradition for the top players to play on the three immaculate grass courts in her garden prior to Wimbledon. It was considered an honour to be invited and an amateur touch before the Championships. I have pictures of me reclining on one of her sun loungers rather than playing tennis!

Life was a whirlwind of congratulations. I received my first congratulatory telegram from Sir Winston Churchill. The England football team, in Stockholm for the 1958 FIFA World Cup, sent me a message. Although I had not been following the team, it is always a bonus when sports overlap. Beating Althea in the Wightman Cup will always be my finest hour.

After a successful British season, and now with wins against Althea Gibson and Dorothy Knode, I was catapulted into being seeded No.2 at Wimbledon. At 17, I was the youngest British seed since the war. Norman was a great philosopher, amongst other things. His mental approach was important to me. He often quoted John Heywood: "Rome was not built in a day, but knocked down overnight." This sadly proved true.

No words can describe my disappointment at being knocked out of the Wimbledon Championships a week later. I went from being a winning superstar to a fallen star in three weeks. Such is the enigma of sport. How was it that a week ago I had beaten the Wimbledon Champion? Had this lulled me into a false sense of security? Like a huge wave, it knocked me down and I did not see it coming. In the fourth round, I unexpectedly lost to the promising young American Mimi Arnold 8-6, 6-3. From being on top of the world I was slow and sluggish. At just 5' 1", Mimi was a chunky pocket dynamo of the future. Her mother had been a former Wightman Cup player. The press recognised my loss as a bitter pill to swallow. For me it was another Wimbledon Championships when my hopes were dashed and defeat was an unhappy letdown. It was called 'character-building' when I attended another Championship Ball. I did not really appreciate that. All the worse since the 1958 Men's Champion was the gorgeous Ashley Cooper. Feeling envious as I watched Althea and Ashley start the dancing would have been an understatement. On reflection, I had peaked at the Wightman Cup, where I had beaten Wimbledon Champion Althea just two weeks earlier.

Beating Althea Gibson to help win the Wightman Cup, 1958

The winning Wightman Cup team of 1958 prior to warm up at Beckenham.
L to R, above: **Mary Halford (Captain), me, Ann Shilcock, Pat Ward,**
and seated **Ann Haydon and Shirley Brasher**

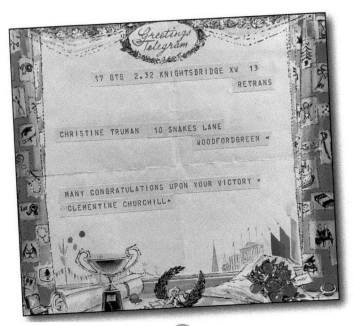

Althea Gibson congratulates me on my win in the Wightman Cup, 1958

Relaxing at Lady Crosfield's famous Garden Party
prior to Wimbledon

Chapter Fourteen

HOLLYWOOD

Surprisingly, only a small team was selected to represent Great Britain for the 1958 summer tour of the United States. There were just the two of us. Ann Haydon, aged 19, was captain and at 17, I was her team. Representing GB, our travel and accommodation were paid for by the LTA, with the regulation 12 shillings weekly pocket money. We were guests of the USTA and well looked after. The British men's team was Mike Davies and Bill Knight, who we met for the US Nationals at Forest Hills in New York. It was good to see them and have their company. Strange to imagine a team of just two girls on their own today, with no entourage.

Ann and I got on well, with respect for each other's efforts to reach the same goals. We travelled to tournaments on the east coast of the US with mixed results, apart from winning the Ladies' Doubles at the Essex County Club in Massachusetts, the first Brits to win this title for 30 years. The draw for the US Nationals was tough. I was pitted against Althea Gibson in the quarter-finals. This time she was ready for me; revenge was in her sights. But I was prepared too, and had chances in our close first set, which she won 11-9. As often happens, she went on to win a one-sided second set 6-1, to complete the match. Althea won the US title to add to her Wimbledon crown. It was some consolation to lose to the champion but I was still disappointed not to be victorious.

There were times when being on court was daunting with the heat and humidity, but in New York I had a fan, a lovely chap who encouraged me to stay focused. This was a bonus. We had met the week before in Boston, where he had been watching me play in the US Doubles Championships with Ann Haydon. He introduced himself as a tennis fan who lived and worked in New York, and by chance he had tickets for Forest Hills. We arranged to meet up when I played there. Being on my own with Ann, we both tried to be independent and give each other space. I'm not sure who was looking after who. It was fun to have an admirer and on one date we went to the top of the Empire State Building and recorded a voice memo onto a special disc. I wonder if this recording machine is still there today. We both said we hoped to meet up the following year. Which we did. It was not *Sex in the City*, but a romantic moment nonetheless for a tennis player still in her teenage years. Tennis did not take away normal feelings of attraction. There was time for both.

New York was full of surprises, not least because Mr Perry T Jones, known as 'Mr Tennis' in the US, invited me to play in his home town tournament in Los Angeles, and also in the Pacific Coast Championships in San Francisco. This was a dazzling invitation immediately after the Nationals. I did not know Perry, but he was keen to encourage up-and-coming players of the future. It meant staying away for another two weeks, but I did not need much persuading. Invitations were a means of playing globally against the best in the world. California was where some of the tennis greats originated and this was an exciting opportunity not to be missed. Together with Davis Cup stars Mike Davies and Bill Knight, we flew to the west coast and Hollywood. Our accommodation was in a plush hotel in Los Angeles.

On my first morning, I could not believe I was sitting next to Harry Belafonte, the Jamaican-American singer-songwriter, having breakfast.

Getting ready to practise, I met Vera-Ellen, a famous dancer of that time. She had partnered Fred Astaire, Gene Kelly and Danny Kaye in classic films such as *On the Town* and *White Christmas* and she had just finished filming with Fred Astaire. We chatted for a long time about tennis but when I told her I liked tap dancing too, she looked stunned and left in a hurry. She wished me luck. I did not know if that was for tennis or tap dancing?

A small tennis group, including Vic Seixas and Ham Richardson, US Davis Cup stars, and I, were invited to the MGM Studios to meet Vincente Minnelli, husband of Judy Garland and father of Liza Minnelli. He was producing a film called *Some Come Running*. Its stars were Frank Sinatra, Dean Martin and Shirley MacLaine. The film was not a great success, but meeting the stars is still a highlight of my life.

Walking into the studio with Vincente Minnelli felt weird and extraordinary. It was a large empty hall, very quiet, with just a few cameramen hanging about. I saw the cast, Frank, Dean and Shirley, casually chatting. It was all so low key. No loudspeakers announcing their arrival as they moved over to meet us.

When Vincente introduced me, I knew this was Hollywood. It was real, not just a lion's head I saw and heard roaring on the screen. My world lit up when I was introduced to the film's biggest star, Frank Sinatra. I thought he might break into song: *It Had To Be You*. He didn't. But I like to think Frank knew who I was, though tennis was not mentioned. When he heard I was from England, he asked: "How does the smog in LA compare with the fog in London?" I wanted to ask him what his favourite song was, not talk about the weather! But I was starstruck and carried on talking about fog and smog as if it was the most normal thing in the world. We both agreed that the fog in London could be more dangerous, with poor visibility. Agreeing with Frank Sinatra was unforgettable after such an unusual conversation with probably the world's greatest star.

That is my memory of meeting Frank Sinatra. He was handsome, medium height and natural. I did not know what to expect, but it was like 'flying to the moon' for me, our conversation was one I will always remember – and of course his famous blue eyes.

After adjusting to the cement surface of LA and, albeit briefly, tasting the glamour of Hollywood, I flew to San Francisco for the Pacific Coast Championships. My preparation must have inspired me, because I beat Maria Bueno in the semi-final, and Darlene Hard in the final, to become the Pacific Coast Champion. For this achievement, I received a water jug as a prize. It was a handsome award, but it proved a challenging object to pack for the journey home. Winning in San Francisco was a successful finish to a busy year.

Motivation came in spades when I found I was now ranked No.6 in the world and No.1 in Great Britain at 17 years old. Norman was right – reaching the top seemed possible. I had beaten Gibson, Hard and Bueno. But champions have to work hard. I was not there yet.

There were no direct flights to London in 1958. We stopped at midnight in Greenland to refuel. With only one runway visible, we disembarked in the snow to a building that was friendly but not substantial. It was unlike any other airport I had seen. There were a few trinkets to buy, made locally by the Eskimos, and a cup of water; no cafe or restaurant. It was the only time I felt nervous flying; there was so much snow and ice as we slithered towards take-off. I wanted to shout: 'Wait a moment! We're not ready.' But we took off safely. Kangerlussuaq airport has no doubt been modernised since then and is no longer a refuelling pitstop. These days there are direct flights to London from LA and San Francisco.

Arriving home in October, life seemed quiet after the razzle-dazzle of the US and Hollywood. Woodford Green could not quite live up to the MGM Studios but my success led to another exciting invitation. I had been asked to play the Caribbean Circuit in January. Life was a carousel that kept going round. Discipline and practice were no hardship for that! I cannot stress how reassuring it was to have a goal ahead to help with the intensity I gave on the practice court. Although Norman never failed to give me a purpose to strive for, to be invited to the Caribbean was a bonus. And Mother didn't do long-haul flights!

World Rankings   Professionals at Wembley

LawnTennis
and Badminton
The Official Organ of the Lawn Tennis Association.

Vol. XLIV (New Series) No 20   OCTOBER 15, 1958   PRICE ONE SHILLING

Pacific Coast Champion

CHRISTINE TRUMAN, winner of the Pacific Coast women's singles title in San Francisco. Playing in her second tournament in California Miss Truman achieved her most notable triumph since her Wightman Cup victories when she beat both the Brazilian Marie Esther Bueno and the American championship runner-up Darlene Hard. The previous week Miss Truman had her first experience of the cement surface in the Pacific South West titles at Los Angeles where she lost in the singles to Thelma Long.

The LTA's newsletter celebrates my Pacific Coast Championship win

Vincent Minnelli invited us to MGM studios to meet Frank Sinatra,
Dean Martin and Shirley MacLaine. *L to R, above*: **Vic Seixas, Vincent Minnelli,
Mary Hawton, me, Dolly Seixas, Ann and Ham Richardson**

I never thought that one day I might actually meet Frank Sinatra

Setting off for the USA tour with Ann Haydon 1958

Talking to Budge Patty, 1950 Wimbledon Champion, with Mike Davies and Mal Anderson, Davis Cup players, in San Francisco 1958

A memento of being a finalist in the US Nationals, 1959

Chapter Fifteen

FRENCH GRAND SLAM

Aged 78, in 2019, I received an invitation from the French Tennis Federation to attend the Ladies' Final in Paris. It was to celebrate my 60th anniversary of winning the title in 1959. I was their youngest-ever winner for many years, and felt staggered to be remembered 60 years later. Steffi Graf broke my record in 1989. All I could think was: 'Lucky me!' There was just time to buy a new outfit, put the dog in kennels, and get my hair done, before Nigel my elder son escorted me by Eurostar to Paris.

On our arrival, FTF President Bernard Giudicelli greeted me with the slightly unnerving news that he was born in 1959 – the year of my success. He must have missed my final then? We stayed at the same hotel as Ashleigh Barty, the Australian No.1 who became French Open Champion in 2019.

Spectating felt strange. Did I really play in this stadium, walk through the same brick entrance onto the same red clay court, 60 years ago, and win? It felt impossible, but then most things do nowadays.

The Roland Garros stadium had changed dramatically. The Philippe Chatrier Centre Court had been upgraded and enlarged. As of 2021, there is now a roof. There were overhead cameras that looked like my grand-children's drones. Electronic scoreboards displayed all sorts of information about the players, including their route to the final. I would have liked to read that while sitting down at the change of ends, with an umbrella held over my head for protection from the sun. How did we manage without that? A huge fridge kept the drinks cold, and was it really a million dollars for the winner? When Ashleigh Barty received the Suzanne Lenglen Trophy, I wobbled. It was a nostalgic moment, a tearjerker for me. Clapping for Ashleigh made me realise that 60 years ago, it was true: it was me standing on the podium holding the trophy.

After the final, life got even better when I found myself having tea sitting next to Rafael Nadal, aged 33, and his team. He was looking very happy, having just won his semi-final match. Rafa saw my Champion's Pass hanging around my neck and asked if I had really won the title 60 years ago. He is still smiling at that thought, when he agreed to a photograph with me. The night was still young. The President held a Legends Dinner at the George V Hotel. This was a small gathering for Grand Slam winners. To be a 'legend' for an evening and be presented with an award to commemorate my sixtieth anniversary was incredible. I could not help but feel proud of these celebrations. When Bernard Giudicelli invited 'Madame' Truman to say a few words, I thought: 'That's me!'
Merci beaucoup, Monsieur le Président.

Meeting the Duchess of Cambridge at Wimbledon three weeks later, she asked if I was playing in the Championships. I took this as a compliment and told her I was hoping to play with Rafael Nadal in the mixed doubles. She agreed I had a good partner.

In 1959, aged 18, I was ambitious, determined, young and living the dream. I believed I could reach over Judy Garland's rainbow where 'dreams do come true.' Winning in Paris did not just happen. It was planned, or rather choreographed, after a chance meeting in Montego Bay with Jaroslav Drobny, the Wimbledon Champion of 1953.

The Caribbean circuit started in Montego Bay, where good friend and former opponent Betty Pratt now lived. When invited to play there, followed by tournaments in Kingston, Caracas, Barranquilla and Puerto Rico, Mother was adamant she would only allow me to go with a chaperone. Betty agreed to be that person and also my doubles partner. The Caribbean was picture-postcard stunning, and it proved a successful tour with Betty. I won three of the five titles with wins over Maria Bueno, and Darlene Hard. Victory in Puerto Rice gave me my most original prizes: a Smith Corona typewriter for the Ladies' Singles, (perhaps a strange choice for the title?) and a Remington Shaver for the Ladies' Doubles. At least they were not items I already had. While staying with Betty, I met Jaroslav Drobny, now semi-retired and only playing doubles. He was famous for his success on the slow clay courts of Europe and volunteered to help me adapt my game before the tournaments in Rome, Switzerland and Paris, the triple challenge. Even Norman thought this an opportunity not to be missed, especially as Drobny would be playing there himself. Not an easy decision, for Norman to accept that I was receiving advice from somebody else.

Like all top coaches, 'Drob', as he was known, was a hard task-master. Every shot mattered. His patience was short, especially when I was aiming to hit targets. Getting close was not good enough. Mother was never allowed to watch our practice sessions in case Drob used language she would not understand. Many times I was close to tears, struggling to meet his high standards, but these standards improved my clay court game and gave me confidence. I had a plan: don't play deep to the baseline, where the baseliners wait. Play short; vary the approach: sometimes long, sometimes wide. These instructions and more were rehearsed, over hours of practice. Hitting and hoping was not an option.

The Italian Championships was first. I never visualised travelling around the capitals of Europe with Mother, but as always she came anyway. We stayed in a small *pensione*, a short bus ride from the Foro Italico in Rome, an unforgettable venue. Strap-hanging on a bus in Rome was challenging but Mother was not put off. She said that travelling by bus was more reliable than the club's tennis transport, which had a reputation of being late, but charming, with dashing-looking Italian drivers. More challenging was the unusual arrangement of hiring a bathroom at our *pensione* for half an hour. This was two floors up from the bedroom. It was a major outing and costly, as we had to pay for our hot water.

Maria Bueno from Brazil was the No.1 seed and defending champion. The Italian crowds loved the charismatic Brazilian. She could do no wrong, so it was a shock when she lost to Sandra Reynolds, the South African No.1, in the semi-final. This was my good fortune. I knew I could beat Sandra, but Maria might have been more difficult.

In the final, I had one of those days when I could not miss. I won 6-0, 6-1, only losing 19 points to become the Italian Champion in 1959. The prize was a real gold medal and £20. As the Olympic Games were being held in Rome in 1960, the medal was a replica of the one being used then. It was a golden moment for me, although tennis was yet to be included in the Olympic Games.

After the excitement of winning my first major singles title, Mother and I took the train to Lugano for the Swiss Championships. Travelling by train was an economic necessity, much cheaper than flying. We stayed at the Hotel Diana, a three-star hotel next to a mountain. Unfortunately, the chairlift platform was situated outside our bedroom window – and it started operating at 5am and continued until dusk. Everything shuddered when the lift started its journey – it was agony. Although I never went up the mountain, I knew every platform on the way as though I had been there.

Lugano was an idyllic setting for my Swiss title attempt. Some players went directly to Paris to prepare for the French Championships, but Drob thought match practice more important. I played ladies' doubles with Shirley Brasher, a fellow Brit and former French Champion, and reached the final of both singles and doubles. In the singles final, I beat the top seed Yola Ramirez 8-6, 6-1 to win the Swiss title. This was my second major win in two weeks. But Shirley and I lost to top-seeded Yola Ramirez and Maria Rosa Reyes in the doubles. Drob was right, winning matches was the impetus I needed before the French Grand Slam. I was thrilled to become Swiss Champion. The prize was a smart Omega watch and £19, plus a decorative musical box from Mother that I had admired in the village. Unknown to her, it played *Never on a Sunday*. I smiled because, with Mother, it was 'Never at all' for me.

Stepping off court after the formal prize-giving gave us just enough time to catch the night sleeper to Paris. All was going well until, collecting our luggage at the Hotel Diana, Mother fell over in the lobby. She was obviously in pain. Everyone rushed to help. Never one to complain, it was always: 'Get up and get on with it!' I managed to get her onto the train and into the bottom bunk of our couchette. The top bunk was a squeeze for me and I hardly slept for fear of falling out of bed.

24 hours later, we arrived at Roland Garros to find Drob waiting to practise. Foolishly, I said to Mother I felt a bit tired. True to form, holding her bruised ribs, she said: "Don't be ridiculous!" This was my first memory of the French Championships in 1959.

Joining Drob on the practice court felt purposeful. He steered me back to thoughts of tennis and winning a Grand Slam. I had now played back-to-back matches for two weeks, apart from travelling, and was apprehensive going into my third event. I knew I needed to keep going – or as Norman would say: "Keep on keeping on!" but it was tempting to play not to lose. I had to force myself to play the way I practised. Practise, practise, practise. Play short, play long, put the volleys away, construct a rally, dominate, be patient.

These constant instructions from Drob gave me a knack for winning. I got through the first week without trouble. Father rang to say well done and promised he would travel to Paris if I reached the final. A rash promise. Could it happen? A tough second week would decide the outcome. Meanwhile, Mother had found her leaflet by Sir Stanley Matthews, the famous footballer, on breathing techniques. She was a fan. His advice was to walk briskly, breathing in to the count of eight, breathing out to the count of eight, and holding for the count of eight. Our evenings were spent walking up and down the Champs Elysées breathing like Sir Stanley. Perhaps it was a lucky omen – but an unusual hobby for springtime in Paris. Was this what everyone did? Mother was not thinking how I was thinking and yet, looking back, I can see it was a huge advantage to have her support.

The second week was difficult. Suzy Kormoczi, the Hungarian No.1 seed and defending champion, looked formidable. She had not lost a match on a clay court for two years. This decided her position as No.1 seed. She had a ready smile which gave her an air of confidence. She was shorter than me but was deceptively strong. I was told she had legs that could run forever. In fact, she was everything I was not. 'Did I need to know that?' I thought.

I was seeded No.2. Maria Bueno, who was always dangerous, and Sandra Reynolds, whom I knew I could beat, were the seeds in my half of the draw. Again, luck was on my side, the luck of the draw would count. Sandra Reynolds had another shock win against Maria Bueno in the quarter-final. It was a stunning result for Sandra and a relief for me. Reaching the semi-finals to play Sandra was a match I had not expected.

In Rome, I had played a blinder against Sandra in the Italian final, but in Paris I struggled, losing the first set 4-6. Was I overconfident? It was a roller coaster. I somehow came back to win 4-6, 8-6, 6-2. The match was draining, the clay surface meant every rally lasted longer, the temptation to make winners too soon nearly lost me the match. But at 18, I had reached my first Grand Slam Final. This victory was emotional. Drob was delighted. Mother was in tears. Father and younger sister Nell were on their way to Paris for the final.

My excuse for the semi-final score being so close was seeing Yul Brynner watching from behind the umpire's chair. He looked the image of the King of Siam. *The King and I*, being my favourite musical, I hoped he might sing *Shall We Dance?* when I won. I did try and catch his eye. Sadly, I never saw him again, so I guess he was a fan of Sandra Reynolds after all. My celebration drink was *Thé au Citron* in the players' lounge with Mother. I had to prepare for the final.

Waking up on the day of my first Grand Slam final was no different to any other. I followed my usual routine: stretching, before a breakfast of orange juice, boiled egg, croissants and coffee. It was our last day in Paris and we had to pack and check out of the B&B. There were no flags or banners saying: 'Christine Truman is in a Grand Slam Final'. In my mind, it is hard to imagine it is not a big day for everyone, but for the rest of the world, life keeps spinning round despite my own significant occasion. We said our 'au revoirs' and went to the club early. I needed to be on site to prepare and, most importantly, practise until all my strokes felt comfortable. Practising before a big match can be an anxious time. It is too late to change anything, but I always needed that gut feeling that things were working well. Some days this would take longer than others. Unfortunately, Drob could not stay for the final. He told me that winning would be my best way of saying 'Thank you!' for all his hard work.

It was strange seeing my father and younger sister Nell arriving at Roland Garros. Woodford Green seemed far away. Having them watching in the stands made it feel more like home. Before the final, Suzy Kormoczi and I were presented with a bouquet of flowers to carry on court. True to her

reputation, Suzy looked focused and strong as we walked into the stadium.
I knew I had to ignore her record, but those words 'best running legs in
tennis' crept into my thoughts. Norman sent a telegram: "Champions
know they will win," and had I forgotten his other motto? "Play the ball,
not opponents." With that, I settled down. It was a close match with long
rallies. I used the length and the width of the court as targets but Suzy
retrieved shots that I had hoped were winners. She never gave up, that was
her strength. But despite her running legs, it was an unexpected victory
against the No.1 seed. I won 6-4, 7-5. Surprisingly, it was an easier match
than my semi-final, and my best win on a clay court. My court instructions
and expertise from Drob paid off. "Ooh, la, la! Christine Wins!" and
"Magnifique Christine" were headlines. It had been a month like no other –
to win the Italian and Swiss Championships, plus the French Grand Slam
was a marathon. By hook or by crook, aged 18, I had done it. A replica of
the Suzanne Lenglen Trophy sits proudly in my dining room with a
photograph of me smiling from ear to ear. The £40 prize voucher
went on travel. No more night sleepers but a plane home.

Arriving at Woodford Green I felt like royalty. The press and TV met
me. There were hundreds of letters, flowers and telegrams, including
another telegram from Winston and Clementine Churchill. Miss Wakefield
from Braeside wrote to say she had given the school an extra day off to
celebrate. I was delighted to hear she was following my career and that the
pupils could mark the occasion. But my most amazing invitation was
from Madame Tussauds wax museum in London asking me to be in their
exhibition. It was an extraordinary reception for an ordinary 18-year-old
girl from London.

**A Grand Slam winner – and
two precious souvenirs**

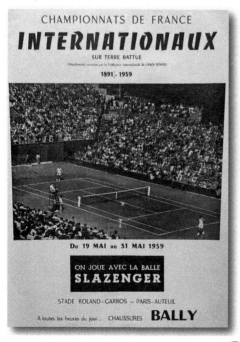

A moment of happiness with the French Grand Slam trophy,
and back home with my proud parents

'14 GTG10.36 AM WESTERHAM TW11

GREETING MISS CHRSTINE TRUEMAN
                    WOODFORDGREEN=

MANY CONGRATULATIONS= WINSTON AND
CLEMENTINE CHURCHILL+

GREETINGS TELEGRA M

Being coached by Jaroslav Drobny in Rome. A memorable encounter with Rafa Nadal in Paris, 2019. He could not believe I was a former winner and is smiling at the thought!

Arriving in Montego Bay
with Carroll and Betty Pratt.
A souvenir, 60 years on,
from my win and return
visit to Paris

Leaving home
carrying my tennis
case to play at
Wimbledon 1959

TELEPHONES:
WELBECK 6861 (GENERAL OFFICES)
"   3726 (EXHIBITION)
"   1889 (STUDIOS)

DIRECTORS:
J. S. RUTTLE (CHAIRMAN AND MANAGING)
B. A. TUSSAUD
J. M. HILL, F.C.A.

SECRETARY:
A. H. LEE, A.C.A.

REGISTERED OFFICE
AND TRANSFER OFFICE
BASILDON HOUSE, MOORGATE, E.C.2.

MADAME TUSSAUD'S LTD.

MARYLEBONE ROAD.

(ADJOINING BAKER STREET STN.)

N.W.1.

Please note change of office address
to: YORK COURT,
ALLSOP PLACE,
LONDON, N.W.1.   CE, N.W.1.

JWC/LL   1st July, 1959

Miss Christine Truman,
10 Snake Lane,
Woodford Green,
Essex.

Dear Miss Truman,

Thank you for your letter of the 29th June. Monday,
11.00 a.m., 6th July would suit our Studios admirably and we shall
look forward to seeing you that day.

If you have any photographs of yourself in tennis kit,
they would be most helpful.

Yours sincerely,

J.W. Catney

J.W. Catney.

THE LAWN TENNIS ASSOCIATION

Patron: HER MAJESTY THE QUEEN

RIVER PLATE HOUSE · FINSBURY CIRCUS
LONDON, E.C.2.

Telephone: MONarch 9051   ·   *Telegrams:* LAWNTENNA, LONDON

4th December, 1957.

Miss C. C. Truman,
10 Snakes Lane,
WOODFORD GREEN,
Essex.

Dear Miss Truman,

Children's Television: Junior Sportsview,
21st November, 5.30 p.m.

I am enclosing a cheque for two guineas
which I have received from the B.B.C. to
cover your expenses when taking part recently
in the above programme.

Yours sincerely,

S. B. REAY
Secretary, L.T.A.

Enclosure:

PMJ/DAB.

Chapter Sixteen

NOT AGAIN!

The Wimbledon Championships were three weeks after Paris and I scarcely had time to wind down, let alone focus on grass court practice. The public's attention was overwhelming. Invitations, interviews and correspondence were left on hold as I prepared for Wimbledon. Mother maintained her usual logic. A good workman never grumbles. If the court is the same size, does the surface make a difference? Her logic was irritating, as I attempted to adjust from the slow clay of Paris to the fast grass surface. I opted to practise on grass, rather than play another tournament. Norman served hundreds of balls and hit me hours of shots in preparation for the Championship. After my success on the Continent, I was excited to be seeded No. 1 at Wimbledon. I learned recently that I am the only British, male or female, to achieve this honour since the war, and I am proud to hold that record still. At 18, it was not a pressure. I would not have known pressure if I tripped over it. To be No. 1 was my hope and all-consuming ambition.

I soon discovered sporting success can quickly turn sour. Four weeks earlier, I was on the crest of a wave winning a Grand Slam title in Paris. But Wimbledon 1959 was a repeat of Wimbledon 1958. I lost in the fourth round, again on Centre Court. I was swept away by another wave, losing to Yola Ramirez, the Mexican No. 1, 6-3, 6-2. She played well. I did not. It was a shock defeat as I had beaten Yola in both Rome and Switzerland. Such is the conundrum of sport. Walking off the Centre Court was an unbearable anti-climax. I had lost. Norman's quote of Rome being 'knocked down overnight' had happened to me in one afternoon. Such was his belief, losing was not a setback but a reason to get better, so that my bad days would still be better than my opponent's good days. Norman always had a purpose to work harder.

Wimbledon 1959 was over. Another year to wait. Feeling frustrated, cross and impatient, I made my way to the ladies' dressing room, where I changed and sank into a long, tear-laden bath. This escapism did not refresh me. I still felt angry. Afterwards, I went to the players' restaurant to meet up with family. The tearoom was full. There was not a seat to be had and no family in sight. It was a tennis correspondent who came to my rescue and gave me his chair. I was relieved to sit down and thankful for his kind offer of a cup of tea. After a long queue, he came back with not just tea but a Bath bun and butter. Naively, I ate the whole bun, spread thickly with butter. The next day, *The Daily Express* ran a giant headline: "Christine must give up Bath buns if she wants to win Wimbledon." In the amateur days, the press were friends – most of the time. Today the Media Centre is in a separate building.

On the way home Father said he had enjoyed Wimbledon. He reminded me that he had missed the church fete to watch my match as it clashed with Wimbledon. "Was it worth it?" I asked. Not waiting for an answer, I said losing was not enjoyable for me. Father was not flustered. His demeanour never changed. Typically, he repeated he had enjoyed his trip to Wimbledon, although not a final, it was a Saturday.

Nothing anyone said would have been right. I had lost. Now I was going home to scrambled eggs on toast. A stark contrast to the atmosphere on Centre Court. It was not a bad loss. Yola Ramirez was a Top Ten player.

What happened? Nothing. The unpredictable is closer than you think.

At home I could not watch Wimbledon on TV; I was too envious to watch matches I could have been playing. My parents did not do emotion. Life carried on. No crying over spilt milk or 'wallowing', as Mother put it. They only knew if the ball was in or out. They had no knowledge of the tactical or technical side of the game. Mother's usual advice was: "Play until the umpire says stop!" All the while the press never stopped ringing, as they knew our home telephone number and wanted interviews.

Maria Bueno won 'my' Wimbledon in 1959. I called it 'my' Wimbledon as I had been the No.1 seed, but she beat Darlene Hard in the final. Maria herself persuaded me to attend the Wimbledon Ball. She knew how disappointed I was and thought I should still go. I wore my new Frank Usher dress bought specially for the occasion, in case I won the Championships. As the No.1 seed, I thought I should be prepared. Mother and I had gone to Dickins & Jones on Oxford Street to buy a gorgeous royal blue straight-skirted dress. Watching Maria dancing with the Men's Champion Alex Olmedo, made me wish I had a crystal ball. Would it be my turn next year?

Norman wrote a letter congratulating me on trying so hard. This was praise indeed from Norman. He was also philosophical: champions lose – but they keep working. No time to waste, no time to dwell on what might have been. After the Ball was over, after the break of dawn, I was back practising the next day. As always, Norman's belief and enthusiasm were infectious.

One of the advantages of sport is the all-important future goals to focus on, and the simplicity of win or lose. The Wightman Cup had been announced and I was No.1 for GB against the US in Pittsburgh, in a month's time. This trip would wind up in New York for the US Nationals. How could I not keep working? The LTA and USTA took care of all our travel and accommodation and still we were given the official weekly allowance of 12 shillings for toiletries and extras. Ice creams come to mind as my extras. There was every flavour imaginable in the US. Do Howard Johnson and the 68 flavours still exist? In those days Howard Johnson was the first ice cream store to sell so many flavours. I never tried them all.

There was a natural lull after Wimbledon before the US tour began. Regions across the country held grass court tournaments, which were the backbone of British tennis, but sadly no longer exist. For many players these competitions were stepping stones to the next level. In 2014, British No.1, Dan Evans, competed at Felixstowe, Frinton and Ilkley, when he was kick-starting his career. He had failed to qualify for Wimbledon, and his ranking had dropped. He needed to compete without the expense of travel. Former Wimbledon Champions Amélie Mauresmo and Marion Bartoli also took part as juniors for extra grass court experience and to gain ranking points. Playing in Britain was cheaper and a way back to building up points for those at a lower level.

Covid-19 saw Jamie Murray reintroduce two British tournaments in 2020, called the Battle of the Brits. These events gave lower-ranked players a chance to compete. Hopefully, this will be the start of more events to follow. It is not a pandemic problem; domestic tournaments stopped long before that. Rumour has suggested it was lack of finance, and 2022 will see a return to more competitions in Britain at all levels. A welcome return by the LTA to help young up-and-coming players.

County Week is another British tradition that has been downgraded. It is still an annual event but what was once compulsory, and an achievement to represent your county, is now less important. Financially, it is not always a viable proposition and sadly, better offers can be more tempting. Surface priority is a current consideration. The format for County Week is all doubles, based on seven groups of six men's and six ladies' teams, the pinnacle being Group One at Eastbourne. There are no umpires or line judges. Line calls could be dubious, and losing the score could be fatal. Suspense lurked, until the final shot was played. The eventual winners were often decided by the narrowest of margins. For me, it was a tennis education of styles and shots not seen anywhere else. If playing County Week were to stop a player from winning Wimbledon, I have to say they probably would not win Wimbledon anyway.

Playing annually for Essex for 25 years, I found that even competing at Wimbledon did not excuse me from playing County Week. When Essex were in Group Three at Budleigh Salterton in Devon, I remember being asked to judge a donkey competition. An unusual request, as I was not an expert on donkeys. They all looked the same to me. But I was told – a spoiler alert here – which was the winner in advance.

After Budleigh Salterton in July 1959, came a rare moment of diversion from tennis. In the post was an invitation from my army cadet to attend his Regimental Ball in Germany where he was based. Our liaison had continued mostly by post, travel making dates an impossibility for both of us. No chance of progress on the romantic front. It was a military operation of MI6 proportions for Mother. She phoned most of the top brass in the British army. But at least I was allowed to go. Most importantly my new dress from Dickins & Jones was not wasted after all.

Arrangements were made for me to stay with the Regimental Commanding Officer's family. Despite being chaperoned, I had a refreshing weekend. The Ball was a success. We did manage to escape from the chaperone for some romantic moments. What can I say? We had a good time. I can't jazz it up any more than that!

In between practice sessions at Queen's Club with Norman, I had to fit in a visit to Madame Tussauds for hair-matching and a selection of my Ted Tinling tennis dresses for my model to wear. Hard to believe 'Christine Truman' was nearly ready. Being a waxwork model at Madame Tussauds at

18 made me realise I had earned this recognition. Apart from asking if they could make me six inches shorter, I began to feel more confident as a person. It was a golly-gumdrops moment when I finally saw my model waxwork for the first time. That's me! I could not change who I was.

Another highlight was playing in a charity cricket match for Colin Cowdrey's XI against Harry Secombe's team. Having never played cricket before, I bowled out Pat Hornsby-Smith, a local Member of Parliament, with my first ball. It was an embarrassing cricketing debut, but after making 18 runs, I was caught out by Test cricketer, Godfrey Evans. Sadly, that was my first and last game of cricket. Juggling fun appearances was stimulating. Unlike today, there were no off-court financial endorsements. With no obligations, I could pick and choose what fitted in with my training schedule.

In August 1959, the Great Britain Wightman Cup Team flew to Pittsburgh to defend the trophy. It was to be held, again, at the luxurious Edgeworth Club where we had played in 1957. The team consisted of Angela Mortimer, Shirley Bloomer, Ann Haydon and me, now proudly, the British No.1, captained by Mrs Bea Seal. Great Britain were predicted a win, but we lost 4-3. The US had a secret weapon in Beverly Baker Fleitz. Beverly had been a Wimbledon finalist in 1955 and was making a comeback. She was ambidextrous, dynamic, and accurate. The only other player I have seen with a similar game was Monica Seles, but she held the racquet with both hands.

Beverly switched hands which was remarkable to watch, and deadly to play against. She did not lose a set. My plan was to play her up the middle of the court hoping she would become indecisive, but it did not work on the slow clay. Beverly, with tap-dancing footwork, changed hands in a flash and dominated the match. I beat Darlene Hard, which was encouraging.

Ann Haydon also won her singles match against Sally Moore. But losing 4-3 was a disappointing start to the US Tour.

After navigating our way along the east coast, the US Doubles were again held at the Longwood Cricket Club in Boston, still as a separate event. Shirley Bloomer and I lost in the quarter-finals. Our tour would now be finishing at Forest Hills where the team was entered for the US Nationals Singles in New York.

New York again was hot and humid, but I liked the buzz of the city and, of course, Saks Fifth Avenue, a leading department store. My fan of 1958 had not forgotten me. We kept in touch via letters across the pond, and this added a bit of mystery to meeting up. Would we still feel the same? Would he still be as nice? It was yes! He was still working in New York and it was uplifting to have his support. It boosted my morale as he was fun and romantic. Cities were much more exciting without Mother!

Maria Bueno and I had our eye on the singles title and the World No. 1 ranking. Three Brits were seeded: me at No. 3, Angela Mortimer at No. 4, and Ann Haydon at No. 8. With Maria Bueno No. 1, Sandra Reynolds No. 2, and Darlene Hard at No. 6, the scene was set. But the draw produced my worst nightmare.

In the second round I would play Mimi Arnold. Mimi had been the reason for my shock loss at Wimbledon in 1958, when I was seeded No. 2. The press reported I had crashed out of Wimbledon when, more truthfully, I had been crushed by a mini tornado. She was 5'1", blue eyes, very cute, and dynamite on the baseline.

Norman wrote reminders: 'Don't think, just do!' But I felt threatened by the smallest competitor in the draw. As I walked onto the Stadium Court, the home crowd naturally cheered and clapped for Mimi. She was half my size, the underdog and American. My concentration became my focus. It was a tricky first set against Mimi's solid baseline play. She gave nothing away until I went ahead at 6-5. This rattled her consistency and I won the match 7-5, 6-1. My reaction was one of relief. I felt as though I had climbed Mount Everest. Sometimes, for no reason at all, an opponent can be awkward and unsettling. Having been fearful of losing to Mimi, I could now look forward to my matches ahead. Without losing a set, I reached the semi-finals of my second Grand Slam.

It is never a good feeling to play a member of your own team, and I was up against Ann Haydon for a place in the final. Travelling together and being rivals was an added tension. There is not much to talk about with a team member when you become opponents. The match was one-sided. I won 6-3, 6-3 and at 18, I had reached the final of my second Grand Slam in 1959. Maria Bueno would be my opponent. We both knew that the winner would be ranked No.1 in the world. I had won the French Championships, and she had won Wimbledon. This was the decider, the outcome being as tantalising as a final could be. My New York escort promised he would take me to see the opening of *Gypsy,* with Ethel Merman on Broadway if I won. An incentive. I hoped I would win.

At the Drake Hotel I was on my own. The GB team had left. I kept to my usual routine: an early night, breakfast, and transport to the West Side Tennis Club in Forest Hills. It felt strange to be completely on my own for a Grand Slam final. No coach, no family, just a phone call from home to say good luck. Mother's words being: "Think how you'd feel if you were not in the final." This was her long-distance common sense. Norman must have run out of ink with so many reminders by airmail. "Play the ball. Move. Don't think. Don't wait. Wait – and you wait for ever." And my favourite telegram: "Champions know they will win."

My abiding memory, other than wanting to win, was that I must not let this chance slip. Keep going. Keep on keeping on. That is all I can do. I had beaten Maria twice in the past year, but we had not played each other since

Caracas in February, where I had won in two sets. Neither of us had the support of a coaching team. Maria often travelled with her brother Pedro. But Sao Paulo, her home, was a long way from the tennis circuit. We were both on our own for the final. Me at 18, and she 19. Walking onto the Stadium Court, I was not nervous. Warming up I heard shouts from the crowd: "Come on, Margaret!" When I was in the US I was often asked if I was the former President Harry Truman's daughter, Margaret. As far as I know Margaret did not play tennis, nor was she tall. I never met her. But it was good to have her fans' support.

Like Emma Raducanu, I loved New York; but unlike Emma, I had not played there as a junior. There was an energy in the city that was irresistible and lifted the spirits. Having a date helped! Norman never stopped writing and sending me telegrams. His words were always in my mind. An extraordinary partnership with a coach. His consistent support and belief in my potential were unusual. I was lucky. Unfortunately, I lost 6-1, 6-4 in an hour. The second set was close, but Maria was too good on the day.

Norman wrote to me immediately after losing. Not dwelling on my loss at all, he said: "Next Wimbledon will be interesting with Bueno, Hard, Smith, Hantze, King and you. Think of a flower show – think of the flower that wins first prize in a flower competition. First of all, the flower bed has to be very carefully prepared. A lot of work. Then the seeds are put in and very carefully watched, fed and watered, etc., etc. Then they are protected against enemies wishing to destroy them, such as insects, birds. Finally, after tremendously hard work and keeping at it all the time, it blooms into a first-prize winner. It takes a long time because there must be plenty of hard work along the correct lines."

This was typical of Norman. No dwelling on my loss but a description of my mental approach ahead. Reaching the top is a feat of desire. Staying there is a feat of desired endurance.

A prize-giving took place. I received a silver plate engraved with 'Runner-Up' in large letters. How I hated those words. Playing in a Grand Slam final is an extraordinary achievement – but losing takes away the significance of how much effort went into reaching that pinnacle. I went to see *Gypsy* rather than spend a lonely evening with my silver plate. There was no equivalent to the Wimbledon Ball in New York in those days, so *Gypsy* was a welcome distraction. It helped to share my disappointment with a sympathetic listener.

50 years later, in 2009 whilst shopping in Tesco, I watched on a TV screen as Maria Bueno walked onto the Stadium Court at Flushing Meadows to present the Ladies Champion, Kim Clijsters, with the trophy. This honour was to recognise Maria's achievement for winning the title in 1959, 50 years earlier. I wanted to shout out across the soap powders: 'Yes, she beat me!' while I carried on with my shopping. Such is the gulf between winning and losing.

Playing at Wimbledon 1959. Wish I could get off the ground now!

Chapter Seventeen

AUSTRALIA

Arriving home from New York I had mixed feelings. While I had not triumphed in the US Open, I did hear the exciting news that I was ranked No.2 in the World. But No.2 was not good enough for Norman, he never stopped telling me I could do better. I could be No.1. That was my belief too. He was totally committed to my ambition, consistently urging me to do better and try harder. I doubt I could have done this by myself. Thank goodness No.2 was good enough to be invited to meet Sir Winston Churchill. I look up to him as our greatest statesman ever, and was proud of the telegrams he sent me. The family used to tease me and say I made him famous, but that was not quite true! He was touring Woodford Green in 1959 as our local MP for Wanstead and Woodford. At 84, it was his last public engagement. His huge, open-topped car was parked in Snakes Lane at the committee rooms, a few doors down from our house. I was escorted to meet him by the Committee Chairman. To be honest, he looked rather old, sitting on the back seat with a rug around his legs. I tried to step into the car to shake hands and nearly sat on his lap as there was not enough room for Clementine, his wife, in the car too. Instead, I stood by his side with Clementine shouting: "Winston! It's the tennis girl, dear!"

I like to think Winston did remember who the 'tennis girl' was as we shook hands. Nothing surpasses shaking hands with Winston Churchill.

Visiting Chartwell, Churchill's home, 12 years ago, the stewards on duty remembered my photograph and told me that both Winston and Clementine had followed my career. I took that to heart.

After this memorable meeting there was an invitation from the Australian Lawn Tennis Association, inviting Maria Bueno and me to tour Australia. We were to be chaperoned by Harry and Nell Hopman. Harry Hopman was the Australian Davis Cup captain and the coach who produced so many champions, including Rod Laver, now the GOAT (Greatest Of All Time). This was an unexpected surprise. Maria and I did not know each other well, despite playing on the tennis circuit since 1958. We had not played doubles before, and she was not an outgoing person, more a proud and private individual, so I felt apprehensive about a tour of Australia together. I need not have worried. We were a solid and successful pair for four months, with never a cross word between us.

My parents saw me off at Heathrow Airport. Father wore his bowler hat for the occasion. For the first time I was tearful; leaving on my own at 18, and travelling to the unknown for four months was daunting. It did not get any better on the plane. I sobbed all the way to Geneva, our first stop. The plane was not full; I had a window seat and next to me were two empty spaces, with a gentleman sitting in the aisle seat.

After Geneva, the gentleman in the aisle seat moved and sat next to me. My first thought was, 'What would Mother say?' He knew I was upset and chatted to me about my trip. I told him I was going to Australia to play tennis for four months and I was homesick already. He explained that he was an author who had spent all his money on researching his latest books. His home was in Australia where he was hoping to hear good news from his publishers. We arrived in Sydney after three days and eight fuel stops. There I discovered my travel companion was Morris West, who wrote

The Shoes of the Fisherman and *The Devil's Advocate*. I never saw him again, but it was good to know he became a successful author as well as being a sympathetic passenger.

Nell Hopman met me at Sydney airport. We stayed in Sydney overnight. Maria was delayed, and I flew to Brisbane the next day with some Australian players I knew. Mrs Wardrobe was my host in Brisbane. But, after a long journey, it was a strange introduction as Mrs Wardrobe was not expecting me to stay with her. She apologised for the muddle, as she already had several players staying in her house and there was no room for me indoors. I wondered what that meant. I soon found out when she kindly offered me a spare bunk on her veranda that I could use. Having never slept in a tent, let alone on a veranda, I did not sleep a wink. I had a mosquito net, but the noise of the mosquitos and other strange sounds from the darkness of the garden kept me awake. I might not be nervous on a tennis court, but I was terrified on Mrs Wardrobe's veranda.

Brisbane was hot after London. I had a week to adjust to the jetlag and then to get acclimatised to the heat. To help, the tournament officials included a trip to the Gold Coast where I tried surfing for the first time. Fabulous! I loved the surf. It was supposed to be attractive to have a tan, and Factor-50 sun protection was unheard of. I used a touch of Brylcreem on my face. I'm not sure why Brylcreem; it was a popular men's hair lotion, but everyone seemed to carry a jar in their luggage. Although I had freckles and fair skin, I coped with the sun on court, but to this day, I have never enjoyed sunbathing.

Despite my stay on the veranda with Mrs Wardrobe, I won the Championships in Brisbane. Fortunately, I did manage to move to a proper bed inside her house when some of the guests had lost and left. This title was a good start, and now that Maria had arrived from Brazil, I flew to Adelaide, where training began in earnest with Harry Hopman. Like all the best coaches, his training was based on a disciplined work ethic. His rules were simple. No one stopped practising before Harry.

His trademark workout was with three players: two at the net against a singleton, who had to get his or her racket on every ball at the baseline. My knees felt they would bend both ways before Harry would allow me to change round. If the ball went wide and was almost unreachable, Harry shouted: "When in doubt, hit a very high lob. A high ball can be difficult to put away and gives you a chance to recover." Volleying drills meant speeding up reactions. If the ball hit you, tough. Don't let it happen again. Harry made sure the ball did hit us now and again!

He also carried a handkerchief in his pocket which he would place in the service box as a target. These targets created angles that seemed impossible to hit. But with practice, surprisingly they became doable. His fitness regime was basically running, skipping and stretching. I had one extra exercise, which was swinging a large skittle in the rhythm of my service action. This improved my serve, generating more power from a better swing.

Maria, in contrast, preferred to do all her hard work on the practice court. She was the most balletic of all tennis players that I had seen. I wasted hours in Australia trying to emulate her style before realising, that at nearly six foot, it was never going to happen. Despite being on court with her most days, we never played points. She was in charge. Her dedication was impressive. Her style looked easy but, like most talent, what looks easy is only accomplished with hours of practice. During Wimbledon, Maria would practise for one and a half hours before a match, and often again in the evening, after her singles and doubles.

Comparing the fitness of yesteryear with today's focus on physical conditioning, is like comparing chalk and cheese. Rod Laver always said that playing singles, doubles and mixed doubles at Wimbledon, plus Harry

Hopman's regime of running five miles around the Serpentine from the hotel before supper, kept him pretty fit. There's no answer to that. But tennis careers last longer today, and fitness is key. I love all the Lycra gym kit in eye-catching colours but just not sure it would suit me now.

Touring Australia was a challenge. Our hosts made us welcome in all the six states we visited. Due to their kind hospitality, we had little free time, but were able to visit beaches, see koala bears, and try out some boomerangs. However, our reputations and rankings weighed heavily on our shoulders. We had everything to lose when we went on court – and nothing to gain. We were targets, and our pride was dented when we lost. We were both bad losers. The Aussie girls presented strong opposition. They had many talented players including Margaret Smith, Jan Lehane, Lesley Turner and Robyn Ebbern, to name just a few. Winning all our doubles matches helped keep our spirits up, both on and off the court.

Playing in the Western Australian Championships, we spent Christmas in Perth. It was in Perth when I received the biggest shock of my life. I still tremble when I think about this peculiar emotional moment. Our accommodation was seven miles from the King's Park Tennis Centre. Harry and Nell did not travel to Perth, so Maria and I decided to rent a car for our two-week stay. This was a practical decision because of the challenge of getting around with a tight schedule. We both had driving licences and did not expect a problem. That was until someone who appeared to be a police officer, attached to the car rental firm, asked me to step inside his office for the 'mere formality' of an eye test. From my left eye I could see nothing. None of the letters on the test card, not even the test card itself, just grainy grey images of light. His report banned me from driving in Australia. I had no licence now. This made headlines: "Christine Truman banned from driving after failing eye test." A strange piece of news since I was invited to Australia as the World No. 2. This incident was upsetting, and the overload of disbelief made me weep. It was not easy to accept and cope with this news a long way from home. But we still hired a car, as Maria had passed her eye test to be the driver. She was now my chauffeur.

Unlike Great Britain, Australia requires a driver to see independently with both eyes. I was at a loss. I never fully understood the significance of this diagnosis until much later in life. It was after information like this that I missed having family around to share the feeling of having something wrong with me. Having known no different all my life I knew it had not held me back, but it still seemed scary to know that I was virtually blind in one eye.

In the distant past, at Essex House School, I remembered we had a talk on the blind when I was nine years old. After this talk, I told Mother I could not see out of my left eye. She said: "Don't be so ridiculous!" and that was that. Nothing more was said. Mother was always suspicious of the medical world since her friend, Mrs Willis, went into hospital with an ingrown toenail and never came out. The family were often reminded of Mrs Willis if we complained of any aches and pains.

Added to the shock of my eye diagnosis, Christmas in Perth was not a memorable festive occasion. There was a Christmas tree with fairy lights in the hotel lobby, and piped music playing carols in the dining area.

On Christmas Day, Maria and I had lunch together. I wish I could remember what we talked about, or even what we ate. Neither of us ever discussed our route to the top, or our thoughts about other players. Maria was not a gossip. She was a private person, but there was always a slight barrier that made me tread carefully in conversation. She was definitely No.1. No doubt about it. She did not gloat and make me feel a lesser player or person. It was just accepted that she was the best and I felt in awe of her talent. We never fell out and, as a doubles team, we were glued together with a respect that lasted a lifetime.

On Boxing Day, the Club Committee invited us to join them for a BBQ on the beach. I also had some cassette recordings from the family but did not want to listen to news from home. It was a tough few days for both of us. After Perth, we played in Tasmania, our last state to visit. It was a brief stay before we flew to Melbourne for the Australian Grand Slam title to be played at Kooyong, the original venue for the Championships. Together, Maria and I had won every doubles title in the six states. Maria was now expected to win the Australian Grand Slam title. She was No.1 seed, and I was No.2. After a shock defeat, Maria was devastated to lose to Margaret Smith in the quarter-finals. It was the only time I saw Maria crumble. She always, but always, kept her emotions to herself. But when she came off the Stadium Court, having lost to Margaret, she was as unhappy as I have seen her. It was our last tournament and she wanted to finish with a win. She hated losing. She always said 'The Last Eight Club' was for losers.

I too was unhappy, losing to Jan Lehane in the semi-final after leading 5-3 in the final set. This was not the ending we anticipated. We won the Grand Slam Ladies Doubles and were presented with a silver plate each from Field Marshal The Viscount Slim, the Governor-General of Australia. We both felt drained from our efforts and it was a subdued ending to our tour.

It was now February and New Zealand beckoned. I regret not accepting the invitation to stay for another month and see New Zealand, but we had both run out of steam. Instead, we accepted an invitation to play two exhibitions in Honolulu which would be on our way home. This was in return for two days staying in a five-star hotel on Waikiki beach, a glamorous taste of tennis life. The exhibitions were not arduous. We fixed the score. We would reach four games all – and then play out the set. Sorry to be revealing a spoiler. In the morning, we took hula dancing classes before breakfast, surfed in the sea before lunch, and tried limbo dancing in the evening with a barbecue. I still need to go back for more practice at the limbo. I never did get under the bar! It was too low for me. This was an exotic finale before saying goodbye. It was goodbye, Maria style, not a fond farewell after our time together, no emotion, no acknowledgement of our tour. Just goodbye. Nothing more was said. She flew back to Brazil, and I to London.

Maria and I never talked of our plans for the coming season. I assumed and hoped we would continue our successful partnership. It was not to be. When I got home, I was disappointed to receive a postcard from Maria explaining that she was committed to playing doubles with Darlene Hard in the future. I knew Darlene had a better doubles record than me, but true to form, Maria kept this plan to herself whilst we were away. It was a shame not to have been in the know and to have talked about our plans for the season ahead. We never played together again, which was sad. However, when I met up with Maria at Wimbledon in recent years, she always loved to reminisce about our unique Australian tour. We were two girls ranked No.1 and No.2 in the world, me aged 18, she 19, who lived miles apart and hardly knew each other, yet travelled together for nearly four months. It was not a holiday. We were constantly in a competitive environment. Being a successful doubles partnership was our saving grace. We were a team, both on and off the court, and proud of being unbeaten. I did play in Australia again but it was never for so long or in circumstances that compared with my debut.

Going to Australia: Father pays for excess baggage!

Nell Hopman greets me on arrival in Sydney

Renting a car in Perth was a good idea, but an
innocuous formality revealed an unexpected truth.
Maria Bueno is in the driving seat

Meeting Sir Winston Churchill was a stand-out moment for me.
Clementine shouted twice: 'It's the tennis girl, dear!'
I hope he heard and understood!

Christmas Day in Perth
with Maria Bueno. On the Gold
Coast, my first try at surfing

Chapter Eighteen

WIMBLEDON SEMI-FINAL NO.2

Arriving home from Australia in March 1960 felt like the end of an adventure. Aged 19, the start of the 'Swinging Sixties' had not yet hit Woodford Green.

Travelling, and being away, had changed my view of home. Being independent was refreshing, but I still needed home support. This was the amateur age, when there were no financial rewards. Tournament winners received a 'prize' which had to be declared, in my case, to the LTA. Being ranked No.2 in the world was not a money earner. I had a tennis career from invitations to tournaments globally, which included travel costs and accommodation, with my equipment and outfits already provided. It was glamorous, but I had no savings apart from the money I was allowed for TV and radio appearances. At the same time, I liked being my own boss. This was hard for Mother to understand. We both needed patience to accept these changes.

The tough training in Australia paid off. Norman had never been keen on my Australian trip. Yet the experience of that tour 'Down Under' had done me good. I won the British Hard Court Championships, beating Ann Haydon in the final. Norman was now keen to focus on the goals ahead. Winning Wimbledon was always top of the list. He believed I could win Wimbledon and the US titles; both Slams were on grass back then. With these goals in mind, we decided to shorten the hard court season in favour of grass court practice. Since 2015, the time gap between the French Championships and Wimbledon has increased. This decision has given players more time to adapt to the change of surface and encourages entries into more grass events for practice both here and abroad. With the grass season ahead, I did not defend my European titles. Decisions such as this were always a gamble and not taken lightly. Hindsight …

First came the Wightman Cup to be held on the old Court One, at Wimbledon, where I had beaten Althea Gibson in 1958. With our new captain, Bea Seal, we triumphed again, 4-3. There was no Althea Gibson, she had retired, but the GB team survived some turbulent matches to win. There were again celebrations at the Dorchester. These grand London hotels added an extra lustre to our efforts and certainly victory gave a glow to the results. We were even allowed a partner, or a 'plus one', a daring innovation. I took a neighbour at short notice, who, not being a tennis player, was surprised to find himself at a Wightman Cup dinner. Apparently he had not seen the match.

Next was Queen's Club, on the eve of Wimbledon. It was a mixed event in 1960. The Spaniard, Andrés Gimeno, beat Roy Emerson to win the Men's title. I beat Karen Hantze to win the Ladies' Final. I was proud to be the winner of my club tournament where I had spent many hours on court practising as a junior. It was not an easy match. Karen was supposed to win and was hailed as the next Maureen Connolly. She had been coached by Eleanor 'Teach' Tennant, Maureen Connolly's coach, who had a reputation for picking champions. It was a real struggle. Although I beat her in the Wightman Cup, it is never easy to repeat the win a week later against such a talented opponent. She knew my game and was ready. Karen later became Wimbledon Champion in 1962. I remember some advice that 'Teach' gave me: "Allow yourself three games at the start of a match to try out a game plan." She reckoned that was enough time to play yourself in and if you were 3-0 down, it was not a problem to still come back. I can't say I was brave enough to try this out.

When the Wimbledon draw was announced, I was seeded No.3. According to the draw, I would meet, oh no, not Maria Bueno again, in the semi-final. Some players choose not to look at the draw, but I could not help but peep ahead. Maria was the defending Champion and No.1 seed. Psychologically, she was the only player I held in awe. Travelling around Australia as second fiddle, I accepted that she was better than me, and this became an unconscious stumbling block. Reaching another Wimbledon semi-final made me feel that I was narrowing the gap. Norman insisted I should not even know who was on the other side of the net. Just: "Play the ball!" He also said: "To win Wimbledon, you must be completely different from everybody else."

Our semi-final was scheduled on Centre Court, with which we were both familiar. After four months in Australia, we knew each other and our games inside out. All the family came to watch, except Father. He was still waiting for the final so he would not need to take time off work. I was not nervous. As usual, I did not expect to lose, and yet my subconscious doubted I could beat Maria. She had the aura of a champion which I did not, despite huge crowd support. Ted Tinling dressed both Maria and me, as both of us were his clients. A new, bright pink cardigan from Puddicombes disguised my doubts. Funnily enough, when I met Dame Maggie Smith in the Royal Box during Wimbledon 2021, she commented on the cardies I used to wear at Wimbledon! It was good to know my cardies were not forgotten. The scene was set. Another Wimbledon semi-final, another curtsey to the Royal Box. These moments I had played so many times in my head. The impact of seeing my name on the scoreboard 'Miss C C Truman', always made it real. Two matches from the trophy. I could almost touch it. So near and yet so far. But I lost. I won the second set – but not the decider. Losing in the third set was hard to accept. Another year to wait for another Wimbledon. It seemed disheartening to get so close.

Maria maintained that our semi-final was one of her finest matches at Wimbledon. She was generous in her praise, but I felt flat. Flat. Flat. There were no tears of anguish when I went home with my voucher for £10. The voucher could be used at any shop or retailer, but was not to be spent on anything to do with my tennis equipment or sportswear because that would make me professional. I once bought a picnic hamper and, on another occasion, a watch. Maria was the best player in the world. I knew that and watched her win the title against Sandra Reynolds in 1960.

Norman was disappointed. He said if I won the second set, why not win the third set as well? If only. I knew I had let him down. But Norman never gave up on me. We kept working. I needed to get better. When Maria danced the first dance with the Men's Champion, Neale Fraser, I admired her ball gown. It was from Issa in fuchsia pink. What, I wondered, would I wear in 1961? Had I forgotten Kipling's famous words: 'If you can dream'?

When reading through Mother's memorabilia, I came across a letter from Brian Sack who ran the famous Sharrow Bay Hotel at Ullswater in the Lake District, where Sir Paul McCartney got married. He wrote to tell me that he took the night sleeper from Penrith to watch my semi-final against Maria Bueno at Wimbledon. He was so disappointed that I lost, that he invited me to visit the hotel if I ever travelled to the Lake District. I regret very much that I never did get there, especially since sticky toffee pudding originated at the Sharrow Bay Hotel. I wish I had known that, as it is my favourite dessert.

Do things happen in threes? They did for me. After Wimbledon, Ann Haydon and I were selected, once again by the LTA, for the US 1960 tour. She was again captain and I was her team. We were older now, Ann was 21 and I was 19, and we were more familiar with the trip than in 1958, but compared with today, we were still young to be on tour on our own. All our expenses were paid by the LTA as we were representing Great Britain.

It was an achievement to reach my third Grand Slam semi-final in 1960. Firstly in Australia, secondly at Wimbledon, and now at the US Nationals in New York. I was pleased to keep up this level of tennis, but achievements are not on the honours' boards. Nor are good scores. There is yet to be a board that says: 'Well played!' I needed to win. My heart sank when my semi-final opponent was none other than Maria Bueno. That old feeling of playing second fiddle lingered. We had a close match, and I had chances in the second set, but I seemed to accept defeat when I lost 6-4, 9-7. My losing semi-finalist prize was a silver tennis ball on a silver chain as a bracelet. After I lost, a silver lining was my date in New York who continued supporting me. He introduced me to Bloody Marys at the Stork Club, a sophisticated venue. I am not sure I fitted in, with either the club or the drink. But Bloody Marys it was, to make up for my disappointment. Sometimes people come into your life and play a role that makes a difference. My New York connection was that person. His support for me made that difference. After I lost the Wimbledon final, he was the only person to write and suggest a couple of tall daiquiris might help my angst and disappointment. We kept in touch, even after we were both married.

Despite losing to Maria again in the semi-finals, I knew she was the deserving No.1 in the world and a truly dazzling star in Brazil. She was as famous as the Brazilian footballer, Pelé. At her peak, her face was on the Brazilian national stamp. She had the use of the President's helicopter and a diplomatic passport. Anything she needed was available. More recently, she was a torchbearer at the Olympic Games in Rio. A tennis stadium was opened in her name. She told me all about these plans and was more animated about the 2016 Olympics than at any time I had known her. Carrying the torch was her proudest moment. Despite her fame in Brazil in her heyday, there were no tournaments in her home towns for the fans to see her in action.

In 1960, the Brazilian tennis association invited Darlene Hard, Angela Mortimer, Ann Haydon and me for a week in Rio and Sao Paulo. This was in October, the off-season, to play some exhibition matches with Maria. The crowds were entranced with their heroine and gave us all a warm welcome. It was a tour like no other. Flying Aerolíneas Argentinas, I can only compare our trip as equal to a royal visit. We were met by limousines, stayed in luxurious hotels, went up the Sugarloaf Mountain and flew by helicopter to venues. I even tried my breaststroke on Copacabana Beach. This was not a success, as I misread the signs of 'NOT to swim between the red flags,' and thought I HAD to swim between the red flags. Lifeguards came waving at me from all directions, and hauled me out of the dangerous currents.

Maria was presented with gold watches and semi-precious jewels for her exhibition matches. As opponents we were not left out, and I have some generous mementos. It was a fairy-tale experience to share in the status Maria enjoyed in Brazil. A memorable trip for a tennis great.

Victory at Queen's against Karen Hantze, in the final, 1960

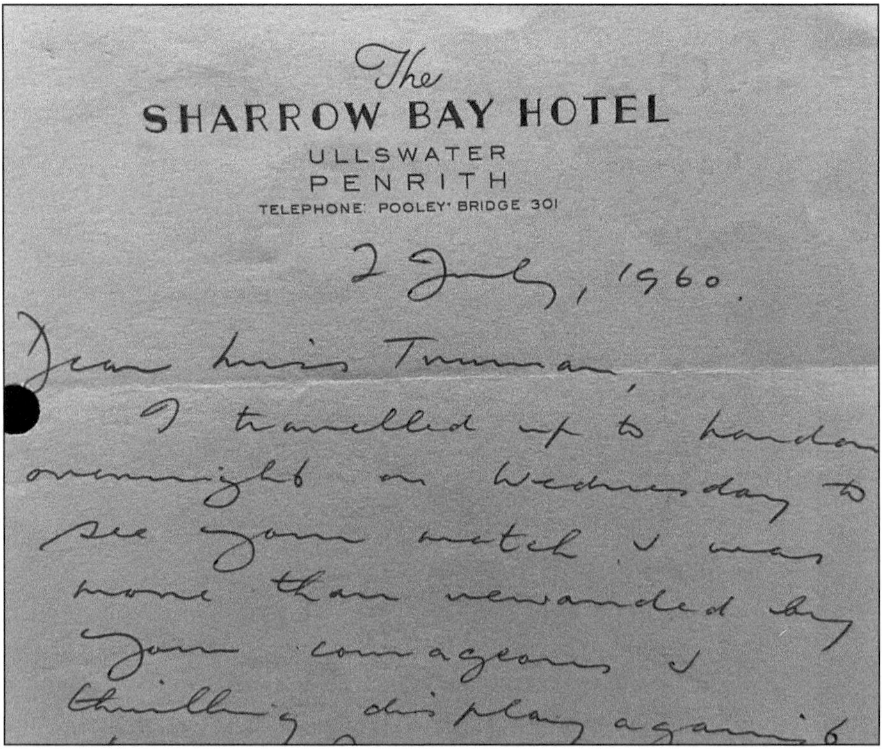

The Sharrow Bay Hotel
ULLSWATER
PENRITH
TELEPHONE: POOLEY BRIDGE 301

2 July, 1960.

Dear Miss Truman,

I travelled up to London overnight on Wednesday to see your match & was more than rewarded by your courageous & thrilling display again.

Brian Sack, the famous owner of The Sharrow Bay Hotel wrote of his disappointment when I was beaten in the semi-final of Wimbledon by Maria Bueno in 1960. He invited me to visit his hotel. I wanted to accept as he was the creator of Sticky Toffee pudding, my favourite, but Penrith was out of my reach

Chapter Nineteen

THE SWINGING SIXTIES

The Swinging Sixties will always be famous as a giddy era of change. For me, it was also a watershed in my career. In 1961, I received my first major injury. At the time it seemed a small hiccup in the bigger picture, but it came back to haunt me. Accidents happen, usually in the most unlikely place and time. They give no warning.

When preparing for the 1961 season, I had accepted an invitation to play on the Caribbean circuit in March. This tour was a favourite, and I felt lucky to be following the sun once more. The first tournament began in Kingston, Jamaica. The club had superb grass courts and unforgettable coffee. It was served black with condensed milk. Naughty, but truly scrumptious. Everything was going well. I beat Darlene Hard in the semi-finals and looked forward to playing the US star, Sally Moore, in the final. On the eve of the final, the British Embassy held a welcome drinks party for all the players. I wore my new red high-heeled shoes with pointed toes. They were the latest fashion, perhaps a bit small, but I tottered along to the party.

The Embassy reception room had a wooden floor. Whilst standing chatting, the left heel of my stiletto snapped through a crack in the floor. This sudden jerk wrenched the back of my ankle and leg. The next day my calf muscle was solid and painful. I had no choice but to fly home for treatment. The diagnosis was an injured Achilles tendon. Rehab lasted five weeks, but regaining my confidence took much longer.

Laid up, I was frustrated at what felt like slipping backwards. Missing the Caribbean tour was a setback. I was now 20, not old, for goodness sake, but aware of time passing. From my first Wimbledon semi-final at 16, there had been no physical setbacks, not even cramp. The hard work I enjoyed had been rewarded with success. Nothing is more motivating than that. Sustaining an injury was not like losing, it was disheartening. I could not go out and practise, there was no simple exercise that could cure my Achilles tendon. Even Mother had no answers. All her sayings were a lost cause when faced with an injury. 'Don't make a fuss!' did not speed my recovery.

It was boring trying to keep fit with sit-ups, and winding my brick up and down for arm strength. I tried doing a Speedwriting course as a time-filling occupation, but it did not grip me with excitement. I could not imagine myself in this role and it became a slow-writing course as my interest waned. Slowly I returned to the courts. Norman quoted: "Two men looked out from prison bars, one saw the mud, the other saw stars." This was apt, but my confidence lagged behind my efforts. It was a gradual process, as Achilles tendons have a mind of their own. I was moving very gingerly at first, which made playing at Wimbledon seem a long way off. But as always, Norman was upbeat. His energy and belief urged me to keep on keeping on. It was quality on the practice court, rather than quantity, as I slowly regained my confidence.

Despite missing the start of the hard-court season, I persevered on catching up to prepare for the grass courts tournaments prior to Wimbledon. This was achievable, although my ranking had dropped due to the injury, I was excited to be holding my own on court again but, by not competing for three months, I was seeded a lowly No.6 at Wimbledon. Although she was the No.2 seed, Australian Margaret Smith was predicted to win her first Wimbledon title, after a winning streak in Europe. The draw revealed our seedings would mean a clash in the quarter-final. Margaret said she didn't like playing me because she didn't know what I was going to do next – and she didn't think I knew either. I called it being deceptive. I had suffered two defeats by Margaret thus far. She was undoubtedly the fittest player I had ever known, hence her record today of winning 24 Grand Slam titles. The week before the Wimbledon Championships, I lost to the new American star, Nancy Richey, in the semi-finals of the warm-up tournament at Queen's Club. It was not a bad loss, Nancy was the US No.1, but I was disappointed. Could I win Wimbledon next week? No one thought me a possible winner of the Wimbledon crown, apart from Norman. Before the Championships started, a journalist quoted Shakespeare:

'*All the world's a stage,*

And all the men and women merely players;

They have their exits and their entrances,

And one man in his time plays many parts,

His acts being seven ages.'

The journalist doubted Shakespeare was thinking of Wimbledon when he penned *As You Like It*. But 'one player' will have their 'seven ages', as they have to win seven matches to become a Singles Champion. He also added, kindly: "Christine Truman was too good never to win Wimbledon."
I dared to believe that.

The 1961 Championships was upon us. Maria Bueno had withdrawn through injury. My routine was in place. Norman quoted from his favourite selection: "Anything is possible, miracles take a little longer." Now that the LTA helped the British players with accommodation, to the tune of £20 per week for the Wimbledon fortnight, Mother and I stayed in a London hotel to cut down on travelling from Woodford Green. She made sure I did not have any late nights. My own instincts allowed no distractions. I was prepared and ready. This was my big chance. Norman reminded me there was no one in the Wimbledon draw I had not beaten. I knew that and tried not to look ahead, but to play one match at a time.

The first week of the Championship fortnight saw all the seeded players unbeaten. No upsets and no surprises. The second week saw me heading towards the World No.1, Margaret Smith, in the quarter-finals. This would be a match between the two tallest players in the draw: me and her. I had nothing to lose. I was not nervous. I relished the support of the home crowd and felt familiar with the Centre Court surroundings. At 20, this was now my fifth Wimbledon Championships and I had already been a semi-finalist twice.

Our match was scheduled for 2 o'clock on Centre Court. Margaret started well. She was too good and too strong. She won the first set 6-3. The match looked predictable. As always I hated that atmosphere, as I did not feel beaten. I was not tired. An inner strength said: 'Keep calm. Be positive.' Attacking more, I surprised Margaret by beating her at her own game. I won the second set 6-3. It was now one set all. For a moment I lost momentum, and Margaret came right back. She went ahead to lead 4-1 in the third set. The final set became the best set of tennis and the best match I ever played on Centre Court. Catching up to lead 6-5, and then 7-6, and saving two match points was a spine-chilling cliffhanger. The applause of the crowd, plus a combination of Churchill's: 'Never give up' and Norman's usual advice of: 'Play the ball!' drove me on. Did I win or did Margaret falter? A bit of both. It was a shock win for me and a shock loss for Margaret. It's still the match I'm most proud of. Mother collapsed in the stands afterwards and had to be helped to the tearoom. This victory brought me my third Wimbledon semi-final in five years. Once again, so near and yet so far.

On paper my next opponent, Renée Schuurman, the South African No. 2, was a less formidable competitor than Margaret Smith. But Renée was having her best Wimbledon ever. She had beaten Ann Haydon and Karen Hantze. I knew I needed to play to win, not hope that she would make mistakes. Thankfully, this match did not compare with the drama of the quarter-final and I won 6-4, 6-4. I was beyond happy. I had made it to the final of Wimbledon. I could almost touch what my heart used to dream of. One more match for the title. To everyone's surprise, I would be playing Angela Mortimer in an all-British final. The first time in 47 years.

Angela Mortimer was 29 and had been in the Wimbledon final in 1958. She was British No. 1 and nearing the end of an illustrious career. She was a deceptive player more than dynamic. It was her determination that made her successful.

The last British Ladies' Champion was Dorothy Round in 1937. Could I hold the trophy this time? It felt so close. Could I start the dancing at the Wimbledon Ball and make the winner's speech? I tried not to look ahead but it was tantalising to think it could happen.

A part of me expected to be playing finals, but thriving on these moments was vital. Nothing changed in my preparations, except Father joined us in our London hotel the day before the match. He kept his promise to watch me in the final. His main concern was whether there was enough petrol in the car to get us to The All England Club. Undoubtedly there is an excitement that is unavoidable on such an occasion as a Wimbledon final. I did not have a mobile phone for company to exchange messages, but often chatting on the phone can be tiring. Luckily, I always found getting to sleep was not a problem. Managing that and staying grounded was important. Making sure the car had enough petrol was an ideal distraction before the final. I still remember these details, however trivial. Most important was having my quiet moment in the hotel, rehearsing how I would play.

Rain was forecast for the day of the final, and it was overcast. I practised and was reassured to find my game was on song. My preparation had been thorough, and nothing needed changing. As always, Norman instilled in me a strong self-belief and I had worked and worked to make my game the best that it could be. Feeling I could do no more, gave me confidence. I was ready. I knew what I had to do. I had played Angela Mortimer many times with some wins and some losses. We both knew each other's game, but I felt the grass surface suited me better. Changing into my match kit for the last time was nostalgic. This was it. This was the final. I wore my lucky Ted Tinling dress with a pleated skirt and of course a new blue cardigan from Puddicombes.

Among the many letters I received was the poem *The Man Who Thinks He Can* by Walter D Wintle, sent by an American fan.

If you think you are beaten, you are;
If you think you dare not, you don't.
If you'd like to win, but think you can't,
It's almost certain you won't.
But sooner or later the man who wins
Is the man who thinks he can.

This was powerful and I was delighted to find the poem in my memorabilia.

The final was at 2pm. I shared Dressing Room 1 with Angela and all the other top seeds at Wimbledon. Two lovely ladies looked after us. Being pampered was part of the magic at Wimbledon. We each had a cubicle for privacy. On the dressing table were Elizabeth Arden cosmetics, Yardley talc, body lotion, hair products, a hairdryer, and nearby, a physio room. No excuse for not looking or smelling good. Angela and I avoided eye contact. It was not the time for conversation. We knew that would not be appropriate. I can only describe these few moments before the match as having an invisible tension. People often ask what it was like to walk onto the Centre Court for the Wimbledon Final. It was a sensation that I can't describe in words. I was excited, but in a controlled way that did not break my concentration for the match ahead.

At 1:50pm, two gorgeous bouquets arrived from the Committee of The All England Lawn Tennis Club. By tradition, these were provided for Angela and me to carry onto the Centre Court with our two rackets, hand towels and even our handbags. On the dot of 1:55pm, we were escorted downstairs by a member of the Committee. In my mind, this was just how I had imagined it would be ever since skipping, knitting, dancing, training, learning from Herbert Brown, Dan Maskell and, most of all, working with Norman and having family support. My ambition of winning Wimbledon was within grasp. We passed, again, through the double doors with the Rudyard Kipling inscription above, and into the waiting room behind Centre Court. I felt calm and ready.

The atmosphere was electric. The crowd erupted in a mixture of anticipation and expectation as we entered the Court. They burst into cheering and clapping for us two British girls. We curtseyed to the Royal Box. It was a blur. As always, I was reassured to see my name on the scoreboard: Miss C C Truman. This was the Wimbledon final. I just wanted to get on with the match.

Unknown to me, Norman was missing. He was too anxious to watch. I never knew. Unbelievably, he sat with his Centre Court ticket in his pocket in the grounds outside. He followed the match from a scoreboard on the outside of the ivy-clad Centre Court building itself. The big screen on Henman Hill had not yet arrived.

I tossed my racket on the grass to decide who would serve or receive. Calling 'rough', the racket strings fell my way, and I elected to serve first. An auspicious start.

"Time, please!" announced the umpire to start the most important match of my life.

"Miss Truman to serve."

That year's *Tennis International* magazine said after the match: "The Women's Singles final was perhaps the most fantastic ever seen on the Centre Court at Wimbledon." It was a strong statement, and a compliment I appreciated. After an erratic start, I took the first set 6-4. I focused on keeping going and concentrating: 'Don't think! Play the ball!' The title was within reach. The sky changed, and it began to drizzle, enough to make the grass damp. I was leading 6-4 and 1-0 ahead in the second set when the referee stopped play. The court coverers moved with speed to prevent the grass getting wet.

Angela and I were silently ushered into the Centre Court waiting room. We sat with the referee. I waited calmly, no nerves, no panic, just aware of the referee's weather updates. I was glad to be in the lead.

Forty minutes later the covers were off, and we went back on court. Playing steadily and aggressively, I maintained my lead. The score was now 6-4, 4-3, 40-30 to me. I was calmly taking one point at a time when I had break point for 5-3. Angela was serving. Victory was five points away when I ran for a forehand, the ball hit the top of the net and, changing direction, I slipped on the damp surface. In a split second, I fell heavily and pain shot up my leg. 'Surely not my Achilles tendon again,' I thought. My immediate reaction was Mother's words: 'Don't make a fuss, get up and get on with it!' As *Tennis International* observed later, it was obvious that I was limping. In hindsight, taking a break would have helped. But with no guidelines or medical timeouts, in what seemed like minutes, I lost five games in a row and found myself 2-0 down in the final set. With my concentration broken, my thoughts were confused. The fall had triggered a fear of my injury. I was distracted. This was the Wimbledon Final. 'Don't lose!' I told myself, I could still win. Angela did not flinch. She rightly took advantage of the situation. Although I regained my concentration, it was too late. Fighting back, I did not dominate the Wimbledon Final again. I had come so close to winning but I lost the third set 7-5. Devastated, I was not the Wimbledon Champion. I was shattered.

The prize-giving took place with pomp and ceremony but I can only remember going through the motions. When 'Runner-up: Miss Truman!' was announced, I stepped forward to receive a silver medal and a voucher for £15 from Princess Alice, Countess of Athlone.

Norman was beyond shattered. Watching the scoreboard, he had not seen in person what happened. Friends and family were sad. Some in tears. But not my parents. They were clapping with the crowd, pleased with my performance since I did not make a fuss and behaved well. Could they not see my tears? Didn't they realise I had just lost a Wimbledon final? The culmination of all my efforts – gone. Another Wimbledon Ball, my fifth, had seen my chances of the first dance pass me by. This may seem trivial compared to the drama of the Championships, but it was a significant finish that counted for me. Making the winner's speech I had planned was not to be.

To this day I respect my parents' judgement. They never changed their ideals, not even for a Grand Slam final. Besides, I was still only 20, so I have to assume they thought I would have many more opportunities. Naively, so did I. Angela was 29, and time was not on her side. But time can play tricks. The goalposts moved as my aims became more erratic and the years slipped by. After losing, I was lost.

Before winning marathon against
Margaret Smith in quarter-final
at Wimbledon, 1961

Walking on to Centre Court
with Angela Mortimer.
Wimbledon Final, 1961

Chatting with Maureen Connolly, my heroine, and Virginia Wade,
prior to Wightman Cup match in Cleveland, Ohio

Winning semi-final at Wimbledon against Renee Schuurman, 1961

Overcoming two match points to win against Margaret Court
in quarter-final at Wimbledon, 1961

Playing Angela Mortimer in the Wimbledon Final

Trying to straighten my calf after falling in the
Wimbledon Final against winner Angela Mortimer

Chapter Twenty

THE END OF MY HEYDAY

There were no media centres in 1961, so a press conference was held outside the Secretary's office in the foyer of The All England Club. Initially, I answered questions from the press as tactfully as I could. Then, suddenly, frustration took over, and I blurted out that I would probably retire from tennis.

After this outburst, 2,000 letters arrived in the post saying, 'Please don't give up!' Our postman had to make extra deliveries, especially for the boxes of chocolates. Fans seemed to know I had a sweet tooth. The letters piled up on the dining room sideboard and the family table was covered with fan mail. There was even a letter from Angela Mortimer's aunt who congratulated me on a great final, hoping I would soon become a Wimbledon Champion.

This deluge of sympathy could not mask my disappointment. The sensation of this loss was unlike anything I had experienced before. There was praise, but praise was no consolation. Normally, I would bounce back and work harder with Norman. But not any more. I realised I wanted a life apart from tennis. Those two aims were not compatible.

If only life was simple. The depressing lesson I learned from losing the Wimbledon final was that life does not always continue along a straight line towards more success. It can be side-tracked, or even go backwards which is what happened to me. When I hear the advice: 'Don't worry! There is plenty of time,' I shudder because circumstances can change very quickly from what looked like a routine path. Losing this match changed my outlook. Despite the many highlights of the 1960s, I never felt like 'Christine Truman' again. My waxwork model would soon be history: my head in Wookey Hole, and my body melted down to be formed into someone else.

It does not take much to become an ordinary player. There is only a smidgeon of difference between the top ten and the second eleven. After the Wimbledon final, my rackets lay idle on the hall seat while I took a couple of weeks off for rehab on my Achilles tendon. My heyday was over, but I did not know it then.

I thought I could have it all. But success had happened back to front. I was 20. Still young. It never once occurred to me that I would not win Wimbledon. But my life was like a maze with so many options. I was lost and could not see the wood for the trees. All those choices diluted my discipline and dedication. My all-consuming sense of direction that never wavered, was too easily diverted. Would money have made a difference and given me more focus? I don't know. With my new outlook, if I had a date, I did not turn it down because of a tennis match. In the 'Norman' days, I would never have been so distracted. For once, I had stopped to smell the roses, and realised that my two-week break was the first time I had stepped off the treadmill for six years. My ambition had been total. I wanted that, but not any longer at the exclusion of a life outside tennis.

Whatever doubts I had after losing the Wimbledon final in July, it did not change my selection for the 1961 Wightman Cup match in Chicago in August. Although I had lost the Wimbledon crown to Angela Mortimer, I was picked to play No.1 for GB, while Angela played a lesser role at No.3. I had mixed feelings. I was still upset by my Wimbledon loss and although I might have the sympathy, Angela had the crown. Was I or was I not No.1?

Losing the final still stung. Reminders still hurt today. Only now can I be proud of what I achieved. Despite GB's 4-3 loss to the US Wightman Cup Team, I had a notable victory over the new US star, Billie Jean Moffitt, later Billie Jean King. Billie Jean was 17, but she already had the star quality of a champion. Although medium height, she played an attacking game, often serve-volleying with quick reflexes at the net. Despite victory over Billie Jean, I lost in the quarter-final of the US Nationals to Margaret Smith, having just beaten her at Wimbledon. It's tough at the top!

Returning home, I accepted invitations to the social activities I had previously avoided. The exception to this rule had been the annual BBC Sports Personality of the Year Award, which in 1961 was held at Shepherd's Bush TV Centre. Although a Wimbledon finalist and a contender for the award, the invitation helpfully enclosed a bus and Tube timetable with two roads mentioned as suitable for parking. I went by train. I doubt whether Lewis Hamilton and the other celebrities know what time the last train home is. At least it was more fun when Bobby Moore kindly gave me a lift home in his rather smart car. He lived in Chigwell, not far from my home in Woodford Green. Neither of us had won an award so we did not talk much. Football fans are always surprised when I tell them I had a lift with Bobby Moore. What? Not you!

During the autumn of 1961, after losing the Wimbledon final, I was introduced to my future fiancé. We met before Christmas in that magical festive season. My eldest sister invited me to a dance in Liverpool where she lived. I had gone to stay with her family for the weekend. It was a blind date when I sat next to a handsome dentist at the hospital dance they took me to on Saturday night. It was romantic and exciting, and tennis faded into the background, despite the South African LTA inviting me to play in the Hulett Sugar Circuit. This idyllic tour started at Christmas. It began in Cape Town, followed by tournaments in East London, Port Elizabeth and

Durban. Hospitality was with charming, welcoming families. The Newton-Thompsons in Newlands, Margie and Johann Barnard and the Tittlestads in Cape Town were just some of the hosts who made this Sugar Circuit special. Although I was training, it was no longer training that monopolised my life and thoughts, hence I was not routinely winning tournaments any more. I missed my soon-to-be fiancé more than I cared about the results. Yet Norman never stopped believing in me and being young, I assumed winning was just around the corner. It would surely all come back.

In 1962, six months after losing the Wimbledon final, I became engaged. I had a fiancé, a ring on my finger, a date to marry and I was in love. Arriving home in February, after celebrating my twenty-first birthday in South Africa, we decided to marry in December. Even then, I doubted it was more than a romantic notion. I was in love with love. It was an emotional roller coaster. My parents were not keen on such a rushed decision and it finally ended when I broke off the engagement in June. Our December wedding was cancelled. This was another disruption to my already broken routine. My failed engagement was no longer just a private affair. I was still in the public eye and another invitation, this time to a cocktail party at Buckingham Palace with the Queen and Prince Philip present, highlighted the downside of celebrity focus. I wore gloves, so afraid was I of the newspapers spotting the missing engagement ring and wanting a story.

The final insult to injury was being unseeded at Wimbledon, a year after being a finalist. How was that possible? My results had not justified a seeding. Romance had derailed my direction. I was going downhill. After a disappointing Wimbledon and a broken engagement, I felt down in the dumps – not like me at all. I took a break from tennis. No longer getting married nor playing tennis as I used to, I needed to work on my Achilles tendon which was still a problem, and I was advised to have more rehab.

Instead of competing on the US Tour, I went back onto the golf course at Chigwell. I was interested to hear during Rafa Nadal's victory in the Australian Open 2022 that he plays golf to keep fit. When the Lawn Tennis Writers' Golf Association heard about my interest in golf, they invited me to play in their Golf Day at Worplesdon Golf Club in Surrey. My best golf handicap was 18. Colonel Legg, the Wimbledon referee who oversaw my first major tennis triumph, was in charge of the event. My experience of competing in golf competitions was nil, and even worse was my lack of experience of the hazards of a professional golf course. At Worplesdon the course had unfathomable heather. When I saw some competitors pinning their cards on a board, I pinned my score on the same board.

Little did I know that only those who thought themselves possible winners exposed their scorecards for public scrutiny. Colonel Legg took one look at the pinned scores: 79, 81, 84 and my score of 132. He handed me back my card.

"Christine," he said, "this is a competition you won't be winning."

In 1963, instead of being centre stage, I was in the chorus line. Boyfriends came and went. Living at home until married was normal for a young girl in those days. Mother's house rules were not flexible or encouraging. Although I was 22, she preferred to know who I was meeting before I went out, trusting in her 'No relationship before marriage' ethos. If a boyfriend came back to the house after a date, she would pull the lavatory chain several times when she thought it was time he left, usually after half-an-hour. Our ancient water cistern sounded like the Niagara Falls, leaving me in no doubt it was time for my date to depart.

Strangely enough, I recently received a remarkable letter from abroad. It was extraordinary, at 80, to hear from a past boyfriend from over 60 years ago. He is 81 and trying to track down the six people who had meant most to him in his life, me being one of them. He revealed that he wanted to ask me to marry him but Mother intervened. He was in student lodgings near Woodford Green and wanted to know if I knew that Mother wrote to his father in 1960. She told him to ask his son to calm down, as he was putting me off my tennis. Of course, I never knew Mother was in contact with his father. Sadly, he still wishes he had asked me to marry him all those years ago. I have to admit these feelings were not mutual but I was horrified to learn that Mother thwarted his efforts. It is hard to believe that in those days, even at 18 or 19 years old, one's parents views were not challenged.

Despite my ranking slipping and my commitment being inconsistent, Norman never gave up. Not even now that my career was faltering. He still believed that I could be No.1, and argued I should leave home to branch out on my own. He saw that opportunities to play with others such as mixed doubles with Rod Laver and later, ladies' doubles with Margaret Smith among others, would be beneficial. Mother insisted family came first and I knew no other way. I regretted my lack of independence, but I had no savings. The £15 voucher as a losing Wimbledon finalist would not buy a flat. My parents could not afford such a move, nor wanted it. It was impossible to leave home.

For Norman it was all or nothing. My success was his success. That was all he asked in return for his hours of hard work. After a win, there would not be even the high-five of today, just a nodding look of approval. He was convinced Mother's influence was holding me back. Not breaking away from home and becoming independent caused our split. There was no argument, no disagreement, just a mutual understanding between coach and pupil. I could not change and we never again went on court together.

It was the closure of a winning formula that could not be replaced. Without Norman's guidance, my tennis was incomplete. He left a gap no one could fill. Without Norman, it was like a racket with no strings. He remained a lifelong friend who was only ever a phone call away. Many years later, when Amanda, my younger daughter, was 12 years old and keen on tennis, I arranged to take her to Queen's to meet Norman. The courts were all booked so they went on to the practice wall. But Amanda did not last very long, because his methods did not suit her. She could not cope with his intensity. Tennis is such an individual sport.

Tennis, as I had known it, had been a vocation. The fruits of that vocation had been a successful part of my life, but now there was this introduction to a glamorous life of celebrity lunches, film premieres, dinners, and sporting functions. Socially, I was busy. With a high-profile name, my presence was in demand in this exciting world. Going to parties was part of the new 'grown-up' me. It did not dawn on me that my tennis was suffering and that this new status had started to replace the driven tennis player. I did not recognise the signs and thought I was 'Miss Clever Clogs' who could combine it all: a new off-court life with tennis success. I was happy being a bridesmaid to an old school friend, an occasion I might have missed had I been on tour. Needless to say, it was embarrassing that there were more pictures of me in the daily papers as a bridesmaid than those of the bride and groom. My name was still a draw, but success was often ruined by the emotions of romantic matches I lost off the court.

Deciding what to do next or where to go was not easy. A part of me still yearned to do what I did best – play tennis. Harry and Nell Hopman got in touch and offered to help me make a comeback in Australia, if I could pay my way out there. This opportunity worked well. My parents helped with the fare and that autumn I started training again with Harry Hopman in Melbourne. As before, we got on well. Harry had a similar outlook to Norman in his attitude and dedication. His intense approach helped revive a habit of focus and concentration. He worked on my fitness and his enthusiasm spurred me on.

Whilst in Australia, I competed in, and won, the first few tournaments in Brisbane and Perth, before returning to the UK to prepare for the 1963 season. I always assumed I would regain my place in tennis. I had been ranked in the Top Five in the world for five years and was No. 1 in Great Britain for four years. Having been at the top, I firmly believed that what I had done once, I would do again. It never entered my mind that I might not win Wimbledon.

Back in the UK, my reputation was still valued and led to invitations to compete across the world. Slazenger, who supplied my tennis rackets, acted as my manager to pass on these requests. It was the first time I noticed that these invitations were starting to add more cash than just pocket money, to cover my expenses. This was the start of the controversy between amateur and professional tennis. It was called shamateurism. Jack Kramer, Wimbledon Champion in 1947, had already started a professional cicuit in the 1950s, attracting all the top men's champions who needed to make a living out of tennis, and eventually Wimbledon became Open in 1968. But the big prize money had not yet arrived. The Olympics became Open in the 1980s, and allowed tennis to return in 1988 when Steffi Graf won a gold medal in the Ladies' Singles. Amazingly, the GOAT, Rod Laver, achieved success both before and after the Open era. There were many greats in Rod's time. It is good to see Roger Federer introducing the Laver Cup in recognition of players before the Open era. Playing doubles with Nell, my sister, we won the first Open tournament, held in Bournemouth, in 1968.

1963 saw my form returning and I told myself that this year, I would be back on top. It seemed my Australian experience was paying dividends. I won international tournaments in Bremen and Berlin before playing in Rome, and then Paris. The topsy-turvy life of 1962 had seen the dust settle, and life at home just carried on. Norman could never be replaced, but his wisdom and discipline were ingrained in my tennis development.

Whilst playing in Berlin in 1963, a small group of players had the opportunity to go to Checkpoint Charlie which was the notorious meeting point between Communist East and Capitalist West Germany. We were escorted by tennis officials for a short tour of East Berlin. It was a silent, grey world, and I was conscious of an uncomfortable surveillance. The atmosphere of Checkpoint Charlie was not uplifting. It was an unusual place to be a tourist at that time.

In Paris, I reached the semi-finals of the French Grand Slam, and later, in a memorable match, I only just lost to Darlene Hard at Wimbledon in the quarter-finals. Something of my old reputation was on display. Top players knew I could be dangerous. But on this goal-driven circuit, I no longer had such a strong sense of direction. Despite my better results, I still felt I was going through the motions without the purpose of the old Christine Truman.

In June 1963, Queen's Club hosted the first Federation Cup. This was a competition introduced for the ladies as an equivalent to the Davis Cup for the men. I played No.2 for Great Britain, and the team reached the semi-final before losing to Australia. In July, I had my first cortisone injection in my Achilles tendon after playing for Essex at County Week. It was a relief after so many injury flare-ups and made an instant difference. Cortisone seemed like a magic remedy, but in my case, it was not long-lasting.

After the Fed Cup and Wimbledon, the 1963 Wightman Cup was again held in the US. It was at the Saddle and Cycle Club in Chicago in August. GB had hopes of winning, but we lost by a narrow margin. My memories of the match are of making history by playing the longest set in women's tennis against Billie Jean King. I lost 6-4, 19-17. This was before the innovation of the tiebreak. Billie Jean remembers that I had two set points at 16-15, but neither of us can recall how I lost them, or how she won them!

In 2021, the Wightman Cup and Federation Cup merged to be renamed the Billie Jean King Cup, a global competition. Billie Jean is someone who epitomises the slogan: 'It is not what you say, but the way that you say it.' She has dragged the women's tour to equality with the men's. Her efforts have made her a legend in sport, not only in tennis. An example of her attention to detail was when I was trying to trace the score of our historic longest set in women's tennis. After trying various avenues, I decided it would be easiest to ask BJK herself. She replied to my email the very same day with the necessary information. This is an example of how she gets things done.

Now aged 23, and trying to keep busy while training in the autumn off-season, I worked part-time in the toy department at Harrods before Christmas. I signed more autographs than sold toys, but the pocket money kept me afloat. In January 1964, I started the new year well by winning the Scandinavian singles, doubles, and mixed Championships in Copenhagen. The prizes were Georg Jensen silver, a classic Scandinavian design. These get a mention as some of my favourite trophies. All seemed to be on track. Hooray! I was coming back, but not for long. Playing in the finals of the Connaught Tournament at Chingford in April against Norma Baylon of Argentina, I had to retire, sadly limping off court with a recurrence of my Achilles problem. After yet more rehab, I recovered well enough to win the famous international tournament in Monte Carlo. This was to be the last time that the tournament included a ladies' event, so I was proud to be the last lady winner in the amateur era and I hope my name is engraved somewhere in the club house. Disappointingly, I missed out on a visit to the casino to make my fortune. Since then, it has become a major ATP event on the men's tour. Nadal has certainly made it his patch, as Monte Carlo is where he starts his unchallenged clay court season.

He has won the event 11 times.

Back in England, my success was short-lived when I had a bad fall on damp grass at the Northern Club in Manchester, a warm-up tournament before Wimbledon. This was not unlike the damp grass of Braeside, but once again, damp grass was my downfall. Like snakes and ladders, my progress went backwards and forwards. With my right arm in a sling, I missed Wimbledon and the Wightman Cup, for which I had been selected. It was intensely frustrating and I started to feel worn down.

Despite my efforts being thwarted, surprisingly I never lost sight of my goal and was still convinced that what I did once, surely I could do again. At 23, there must be time.

My parents helped me celebrate
my 21st birthday with a party at
The Roebuck Hotel, Buckhurst Hill, Essex

Dennis Compton, Bobby Moore and I choose a winning entry in a competition

Chapter Twenty-One

A NEW BEGINNING

In 1965, I made further strides towards my ambition. Could this be it? My year started with a win on the covered courts of Helsinki. After wearing a thick bobble hat in Finland, my next stop was the heat of Johannesburg. Playing at the Ellis Park Stadium, I won the South African ladies' singles and doubles Championships. These results were encouraging, and winning gave me a reminder of my old self. Travelling as far as this included a trip to what was then Rhodesia, now Zimbabwe. I was invited to play exhibitions with three other internationals: Donald Dell, who became US Davis Cup captain, and the South African team of Quinton Pretorius and Pat Walkden, later Pat Walkden-Pretorius. The four of us played matches for a week in return for our travel and accommodation.

There was even an invitation to play in the Kampala Championships in Uganda. The club president rang me and said: "Just pop by via Salisbury on your way." It was not as simple as that, as I had to complete our trip to Rhodesia first. One of my dreams was to see the sights of all the countries I visited whilst competing. These days it is a case of 'Dream on, Christine!' Sightseeing was not normally possible. Tennis came first, but on this trip part of our invitation included seeing some of the tourist attractions. Victoria Falls was breathtaking. But I was not so keen on the wooden raft that took us up the Zambezi River. It seemed very frail compared with the hippos which we passed en route. A bit too close for comfort, with their bulging eyes frequently surfacing above the water to have a look at us. I did go on to Kampala and won the Championships. There was not much competition and few matches, but it was good to have a win.

Significantly for me, I reached the Wimbledon semi-finals for the fourth time. I was back, playing on Centre Court. Getting there felt like a triumph over adversity. Winning a quarter-final cliffhanger against the American No.3 seed, Nancy Richey, was history repeating itself: it was reminiscent of my quarter-final against Margaret Smith in 1961. Nancy was a business-like player. Short and strong, she wore a peaked cap and gave little away, both in her manner and in unforced errors. Even after losing, she never let her demeanour slip. I was delighted to see the headline: "Christine back in the elite." A tear-jerker. It was now four years since I lost the Wimbledon final. Those four years were not unlike being in the wilderness, where life is about learning rather than regrets, but I did not expect to lose my way so abruptly.

Also that year, my sister Nell and I reached the quarter-final of the Ladies' Doubles at Wimbledon. It was an exciting time for us sisters and the family. I was also playing mixed doubles with my brother Humphrey. We got on well, but at the back of my mind was an awareness of Mother's policy that the family comes first. Her focus was on family rather than titles.

Losing to Margaret Smith in the semi-final was not an unexpected loss. Her game was a class or two above mine. She was now head and shoulders above the rest of the field and went on to win 24 Grand Slam titles, a record that still stands today. Undoubtedly, this was achieved through her exceptional dedication and hard work. Her game was built like a machine that never breaks down. Her speed of foot was cheetah-like. She never took time out, but played, week in and week out, never losing throughout the entire season. I lost to a great champion. She received a voucher for

£25 and a replica of the Venus Rose Bowl, while I carried off my bronze medal and a voucher for £10. The prize money had not changed in the eight years since my first semi-final in 1957. Serena Williams is close behind Margaret, with 23 Grand Slams, but time is not on her side, despite her monumental attempts to catch up.

Margaret and I were good friends and often travelled to the same tournaments. Once we were invited to the stunning La Jolla Club in San Diego to train for a week. This was in return for playing doubles with some of the club members. An example of her dedication was made clear on our first morning, when Margaret woke me at 6am to go for a light run. We headed to the beach and I lost her for over an hour when she ran out of sight. That was not a light run for me. Fitness was her particular strength. Rumour had it she could run the qualifying time for the Australian Olympic sprint team. Hence her speed around the court.

After my boost of reaching the semi-final at Wimbledon, I had great hopes of doing well in New York at the US Nationals. As always, I looked forward to New York although my date was now married! But bad luck dogged me. With no warning, I had an emergency appendectomy and could not continue. This was a knock-out blow after my Wimbledon headline of 'Christine back in the elite.' It was not to be. Life seemed unfair. During my convalescence in New York, I stayed with Gladys Heldman. Gladys was a pivotal character in women's tennis and a kind hostess. She made me welcome despite her busy life. In the 1960s she promoted the women's game and worked to create a separate women's circuit in 1970, known as the Virginia Slims Tour. When the game went Open and the women received less prize money than the men, she fought to redress this balance with the legendary Billie Jean King, who took over the mantle of women's tennis.

The injury to my Achilles tendon in my left ankle never fully recovered.

In 1966, I had it repaired with a successful operation at St Margaret's Hospital, Epping. The surgeon told me that as a result of his handiwork, it would be stronger than my right ankle. His prediction has proved true. To this day, I have never even felt a twinge. While recovering from surgery, I worked at Simpsons, the famous sports store that was once in Piccadilly. Simpsons was known for helping injured sports players to keep financially supported when out of action. Mother was not keen on this decision. She wanted me to recover at home where she was in charge, but I stuck to my guns. I think she sensed I was on the verge of stopping and saw me and sister Nell as a partnership. A reason to keep playing.

Taking the Tube to Piccadilly Circus for a 9am start was a rare taste of commuting life. Not getting a seat at peak time was a very different experience from the predictability of tennis practice. I became an internal secretary. At last my Speedwriting course came in useful, but when I was assigned to Mr Creed on the second floor for DAKS, he was not impressed with my typing speed! My greatest achievement at Simpsons was mailing a sailing jumper to Sir Francis Chichester. Yet Mr Creed was kind and suggested that I could come back to Simpsons if my tennis hopes did not work out. I valued working at the store. It was a chance to sample a different kind of life.

Returning to routines of old, I strove to regain my old tournament-winning self, with circuit training, service practice and, most importantly, seeing the ball off the racket. I played a reduced schedule. Fan mail expressed hopes for future Wimbledons, and the celebrity invitations continued to arrive, but my results and standard were mediocre. I was still good enough to compete, but started to doubt I could be that special player again. However hard I dug, it was not enough. After the struggle of the early 1960s, I was disillusioned. Facing the truth, I knew the opportunities to achieve my highest aims had gone. F is for Fail. My failure was staring me in the face. I would not win Wimbledon nor feel like Christine Truman again. This was a confusing stage. What should or could I do next? Would coaching be enough? I needed to work, and part of me wanted to do a proper secretarial course, and go back to Simpsons. I am not sure I was secretarial material. My parents persuaded me it would be more beneficial to help Nell up the tennis ladder. I did, with mixed feelings, as the old 'me' was missing. But family came first and financially, I could stay at home without any major changes. Nell and I had some great moments and success. Humphrey and I reached the quarter-finals of Wimbledon and later Nell, with her bubbly personality, did strike out successfully on her own.

Timing is everything. It was an off-court meeting that changed my life. Before Christmas 1966, Woodford Rugby Club was holding a 'hop'. This was a gathering of local rugby clubs for a social evening, with loud music and plenty to drink. I went with my older brother Philip.

Gerry Janes, at 31, had just retired from playing rugby for Wasps, and also went to the party. I was almost 26 and winding down my tennis commitments. We were introduced by a mutual friend, who was later an usher at our wedding. We clicked over sport. He lived in Gidea Park, not far away and had played rugby that afternoon. I hadn't watched the match as I wasn't that keen on rugby but after a lot of dancing he asked for my phone number. He was tall, we had much in common and he promised to ring me on Thursday evening. Ever the romantic, I was sitting by the phone. It rang. It was Gerry…

It was the end of one ambition, and the beginning of another. Perfect timing for the next 53 years.

A comeback victory against Nancy Richey, US No.1,
on Centre Court to reach my fourth semi-final, 1965

With sister Nell, playing Ladies' Doubles in 1968
at Bournemouth winning the first Open title

Roy Emerson congratulates me on winning
the Marlboro Sports Award for 1965

Chapter Twenty-Two

THE BBC

After the Rugby Club hop, I told the family I had met Mr Right. Jokingly, they suggested he might be looking for Miss Right. Despite those doubts, our first date was supper at the Prospect of Whitby, a pub in East London. Tennis was not a game Gerry played, but he was soon converted, although rugby and cricket came first.

We married in December 1967. I was 26 and Ted Tinling generously made my stunning wedding dress. The material was silk dupion, with the exquisite detail of lilies of the valley. These were Ted's speciality. Speaking at our wedding, Father said marriage was all about 'give and take'– he gave, and his wife took. That sounded like good advice.

Our married life started in familiar territory. We moved into a small flat in Loughton where I found two jobs: teaching tennis and PE. These were at Braeside, my old school, and at nearby Loughton High School. Coaching was to be my forte for the future. Passing on tennis knowledge gave me confidence, although working at a school as an unqualified teacher, I was paid less!

Over the last 50 years, that coaching experience has been life-changing. It has been uplifting to give something back to a sport that has given me so much. This is through all the people I have met by being involved with the game, be it coaching, acting as a referee, or just 'being there'. It has been rewarding to try and make a difference. Although deep down I know I could never equal the help I had to make my career happen.

My active tennis life did not stop completely. Without computer points in the amateur game, I was still able, and good enough, to dip into tournaments in Britain while playing doubles with Nell. In hindsight, it was a pointless exercise. What was I doing? These days, 27 is no age. As well as being a tennis player, my other ambition was to have a family. I can relate to the professionals being tempted to go on just a bit too long. It's a job these days, but the adrenaline of competition is also compelling and hard to replace. As a competitor, win or lose, there is always a new goal next week and the next, but these goals that were once possible, become elusive. They don't return. It is a difficult adjustment for all sports people who have given up valuable years for their success, while their counterparts have been establishing a career that is longer-lasting. There is no easy transition. Having a young family was life-changing for me. Four children presented more of a challenge than tennis! I always wanted six children, but Gerry was not so keen. No rest days, no weekends off, no winter sunshine breaks, no immediate signs of knowing if their upbringing would be rewarding. It was, but only about 20 years later. I could always put my rackets away in a cupboard for a weekend off – but not the children. Having a chance to pursue a life at the top in sport and having a family were my two ambitions. I was lucky.

In 1974, my memorable exit from Wimbledon was playing Martina Navratilova in the first round of the Championships on the old Court One. I was 31 and she was 16, playing her first Wimbledon. This was history in reverse. When I was practising before the match, Virginia Wade warned me this Czech girl with the unpronounceable name was dangerous. Warning me was not enough. Martina was stronger and quicker than anyone I had ever played before, even Margaret Court. I did not know then that I had lost to an all-time great, 6-4, 6-4. She tells me today that she did not want to lose to an old lady. Thanks, Martina! Martina Navratilova, Serena Williams, Margaret Court, Steffi Graf, Chris Evert and Maria Bueno are my top six lady Champions. At the opening of the new roof on Court No.1 in 2019, Martina was taking part in the celebrations and generously mentioned she had beaten me on the old Court No.1. It had been her first Wimbledon and she acknowledged that when I played her I was a new mother, and not quite so fit. Words kindly spoken.

In my thirties I enjoyed the fringe of the tennis world. Coaching and practising with promising youngsters always made me feel useful. Playing club matches and county tennis also kept me fit and involved. I captained Essex Ladies for 10 years. My most memorable effort for the team was playing doubles at County Week, in Group Two, at Cromer. On the final day, winning was crucial. I was expecting my fourth child and, trying to be discreet, I wore a huge girdle to hide my bump, but it was a heatwave, and I had to remove my girdle at the back of the court. Not so discreet or elegant, but it was worthwhile when Essex was promoted to Group One. County Week produced a competitive edge that meant everyone gave their all – girdles or not.

A few au pairs came and went, so I could fit tennis around family life, but when I started working on BBC radio in 1974, my contract paid for a nanny for a month. Fantastic. Gerry often took charge at weekends, but like my own father (my two role models), he was not domesticated. Similarly, they both did the washing up in cold water, a minor blip in the bigger picture, but enough to put off willing drying-uppers! Cold water never did remove grease. On one occasion, I had accepted to play a club match at The All England Club on a Sunday morning. This was a treat for me to have some time away from the children and visit the Club. Leaving no stone unturned, I left our roast lunch of meat, potatoes and veg, in a roasting tin next to the oven, which I had left switched on. All Gerry needed to do was put the roasting tin in the oven at 12 o'clock, but when I returned home, I found it stone cold. He had put the roasting tin in the drawer at the bottom of the oven. Not a real crisis, but it felt like one at the time. Family hiccups could fill another book.

Veterans' Tennis has since become a popular worldwide activity for all age groups over 40. The Legends Circuit draws huge crowds. Mansour Bahrami and John McEnroe never fail to be an entertaining duo. Popular as it is, it did not appeal to me. I hated being bad at something I had tried so hard to be good at. It was just not enjoyable for me, and a veteran with varicose veins was not a draw card.

Coaching was different. I felt helpful. For nostalgia, I look at Martina Navratilova who is still playing competitively at 65. A great role model for the ladies' game. The only occasion I weakened was for a match with my good friend Shirley Brasher. She persuaded me to play for Queen's Club, where I was now an honorary member, against the Purley Tennis Club in Surrey.

When we arrived, our opponents, two sisters, greeted us. In disbelief, they asked to shake my hand. They could not conceal that they were ball girls when I had beaten Althea Gibson in the Wightman Cup in 1958. My heart sank; Shirley and I started badly and got worse. We lost. I imagined the winners were wondering why they were not playing in the Wightman Cup team if they could beat us! Travelling home together, I turned to Shirley and said with feeling: "I cannot do that again."

Typical of Shirley, she said: "Next time might be better."

But there was never a next time. Shirley has stayed my closest friend in tennis and until recently, unlike me, an avid match player.

Five years later, she asked me to play some social tennis at the Vanderbilt Tennis Club in London. I could not get a babysitter for the children, so I bribed them with a large High Tea and maybe a chance to see Lady Diana Spencer, as it was her club. When we arrived, there she was, standing chatting informally with friends, wearing tennis kit. The children ran straight past. They never even noticed her. I said: "Did you see Lady Di?" "No! Where was she?" they responded. "She wasn't wearing a tiara!" No, I explained that she took that off to play tennis.

Walking into the Wimbledon Championships in 1974 as a spectator, I bumped into a radio presenter from the World Service. The BBC began presenting Wimbledon on the radio in 1927 and, on TV, from 1937. Often, they use ex-players as expert commentators. I had never seen myself as taking part and there were no agents to lend a helping hand. On being invited to the TV Studios, I met Slim Wilkinson, Executive Producer of TV and Radio Sport. Slim asked me to have a trial on radio at the Eastbourne Ladies' Championships, which was the week before Wimbledon. He made sure I knew the basic rules: never speak when play is in progress, and never expand unnecessarily. I never looked back. I loved the job on radio.

I worked for 34 years for the BBC, covering Eastbourne, Birmingham, Queen's, and Wimbledon. It gave me a fund of amusing stories. Never a day passed without some hilarity. But it was witty conversation within the radio team that I remember, rather than anecdotes to pass on. At Wimbledon, the BBC supplied us with rucksacks containing books of statistics. I also used these bags for party shoes and a big bag of pick-and-mix. The team had a weakness for fudge. As a summariser, I used my knowledge and felt confident from past experience.

Each day in the radio box at Wimbledon was a working holiday for me. When I arrived at the studio, the producer held a meeting at 11am to give us a rough guide as to which matches were being covered in the programme. There were a number of separate radio teams, allocated to different matches. Max Robertson and I were usually together as the older, and dare I say it, more mature team members. Once the programme was under way there was room for much ad-libbing. Radio covered play on more courts than TV and our programme was flexible enough to concentrate on the most exciting matches as they happened. There were the serious moments too, picking up the on-court drama of a match, and tuning into an unexpected loss. The commentators were fed their statistics and did the ball-by-ball commentary which was exhausting. Being a former player, I was expected to add my opinion on the tactics players were using, and react to the scoreline. This was usually at the change of ends or interjected with a short explanation between points, if needed. From the standpoint of someone who had 'Been there, done that', I felt able and enjoyed bringing my experience to a wider audience.

While breast-feeding my younger daughter, morning and evening, it was possible to drive to Wimbledon and be back in time for the night feed. Mother always told me she never used bottles with six children, so neither dare I, with four! But one morning I felt rotten. I asked husband, Gerry, if he could help by driving me to Wimbledon. Gerry was doubtful. He worked for Taylor Woodrow, the civil engineers, as a chartered secretary to Frank Taylor at the head office in Park Lane. He insisted I rang Lord Taylor's office myself to explain that he might be late. This was not a request Gerry would normally make. He was never late. I rang the office at 8am, and to my dismay, Lord Taylor himself answered the phone. Despite my embarrassment, he was delighted to solve the problem. I managed to catch up on my sleep as Gerry drove me the one and a half hours to

Wimbledon. This gesture was a saviour.

Talking off-the-cuff on the radio, there were plenty of opportunities for gaffes. Once, a less-informed guest asked me if I had played against Suzanne Lenglen, the great French tennis star of the 1920s. Did I look that old? This was not a morale booster. I was at my most restrained when I replied that I had not played before the war. On another occasion, in front of the nation, I misheard Bono, the pop star, as the maker of the dog food, Bonios. But there were compensations. Talking to the great golfer, Jack Nicklaus, I told him I was no good at putting. After a pause he replied: "Neither am I." My putting improved after that, knowing I had something in common with Jack Nicklaus. Watching a set of tennis with Tom Hanks, I found it hard to concentrate on the match.

During the warm-up tournament at The Queen's Club, I heard that Wimbledon Champion, Stefan Edberg, wanted to pop in to watch the final, having won the title there in 1991. The Steward on duty at the gate asked his name as he did not have a pass to enter. Stefan said 'Edberg'. The Steward phoned through to the Clubhouse and said he had someone called 'Ed Berg' wanting to come into the Club!

Björn Borg was a game-changer for me. He was the first male tennis player to only play singles, and the first to have pop-star appeal. His style was that of a brick wall, but with charisma. He made playing with little expression look easy. His coach, Lennart Bergelin, looked the same, watching from the player's box. No fist pumps. Nothing. Rumour has it, Björn practised for two weeks, six hours a day on grass in preparation for Wimbledon. His rival, John McEnroe, was a surprise semi-finalist at 16. He had not yet coined his catchphrase, 'You cannot be serious!' Ken Rosewall was a heartbreaker, when he reached the finals for the fourth time at 39, only to lose to the swashbuckling Jimmy Connors.

The Williams sisters have to be a unique story in women's tennis.

Around the year 2000, I was on the All England Club Committee and had access to the ladies' dressing room. Before one of Serena's finals, I popped in to hang up my evening dress. While powdering my nose, Serena came over and asked politely if I would move my dress as it was hanging in her lucky cubicle. I did not tell Serena we had superstition in common and I was impressed with her respectful manner. Incidentally, their father, Richard Williams, was a surprise fan. He always told me I could win Wimbledon, despite his daughters both playing in the Championships! I was impressed he knew enough tennis history to even know who I was and was flattered he still thought that I could win the Championships!

Working on radio was a wonderful opportunity to watch the greats in action. Every champion has something different about them, a mannerism and a style that distinguishes who they are. Chris Evert had the first two-handed backhand I ever saw. When she was playing in her first Wightman Cup match in Cleveland Ohio, she had a pocket in her dress for the spare ball.

Steffi Graf had the footwork of a gazelle. Martina Navratilova, a superior all-court game. I could go on. I loved being immersed in the atmosphere of somewhere I had been myself, and much enjoyed meeting up with the players I knew of old. Spectating annually in this way was a natural continuation of my tennis life. Following the matches at Wimbledon for the BBC was the icing on the cake. But the definition of devotion has to be husband Gerry who, after he retired, listened to me in Car Park 3 on the car radio. He had tickets but preferred hearing my voice than watching the real thing. At least I knew someone was listening.

In 2008, 34 years later, I was still broadcasting. It was a bonus. The same nanny came every year to look after the children, even after they had grown up. She liked it so much. Producer Bob Burrows started the new

Radio 2 programme, *Live Wimbledon Tennis*, from 2pm to 7pm every day. I was surrounded by experts. Household names like Des Lynam, Tony Adamson, John Motson, Frew McMillan, David Lloyd, Max Robertson, Norman Cuddeford, and of course the great Fred Perry. We were a popular team. Our rapport and banter became well known with listeners. Comic moments seemed to happen to me. My shopping list was mistakenly read out on air: "Can you get potatoes, a loaf of bread, sugar and dog food before the shops shut at five?" I did not know my microphone was switched on when I phoned home.

During a long five-set Men's Doubles Final, an exhausted Max Robertson turned to me and asked: "Who do they play in the final, Christine?"

I replied: "Max, this IS the final."

When introduced to Marmaduke Hussey, Chairman of the BBC, I offered him a piece of fudge, a favourite of mine. He surprised me by saying he already had some toffees which he kept in his artificial leg. I did not fancy one of those, but it was a pleasant surprise to share a liking for sweets with the Chairman.

Working on Radio 2 was the nearest I got to the red carpet. There were special guests every day. Pierce Brosnan popped in for a coffee. I sadly missed seeing Joyce Grenfell, but Chris Evans came into the studio for a chat. The late James Hunt was a heart-throb. I was commentating on Court 3 when the producer said: "James Hunt is here today." I said: "Surely not THE James Hunt?" And with that, the producer immediately put me on air talking to the great man himself. Covered in confusion, I asked him if he had driven to Wimbledon. He had, but not in his Formula One car!

Going home after the heady, happy days of Radio 2 was an anti-climax. Temporarily, family life was mundane in comparison. Bob Burrows,

Dave Gordon and Joanne Watson were producers of quality. John Inverdale, Clare Balding, Jonathan Overend and Ian Carter were some of many who joined the radio team for the Wimbledon fortnight. It was a feel-good get-together, and will always remain a special time in my 'after-tennis' life.

After 34 years, it was time to move on. A new producer arrived. It was in with the new, and out with the old traditional style. Nothing stays the same for ever. And so ended my career in the commentary box. I could not grumble after all those years. Family and friends wondered how I would feel about being at the Championships without the BBC. And so did I. But the magic of Wimbledon gave me time to meet up with friends, guests and sit in the Royal Box. Funnily enough, my confidence was stirred but not shaken.

On two occasions, when I met the Queen, she spoke about my successful radio broadcasts. I could not finish with a better audience than that.

Gerry Janes and I married in 1967; we hoped the police
enjoyed the occasion as much as the large crowds at the wedding.
Gerry is standing with Rev. Kenneth Vine and best man Andy Hurst

JANUARY 1968
TWO SHILLINGS

TENNIS PICTORIAL

INTERNATIONAL

Commentating on Centre Court for BBC Radio

Celebrating at Wimbledon with Rod Laver in 2019.
It was 50 years since he won the title

After my competitive playing days, I concentrated on coaching and bringing up a family. Nigel, my first-born, was soon on court at nine months. Daughters Caroline and Amanda, aged eight and four, getting ready for a game with mum

Clockwise, from top left: Caroline, Nigel, baby Amanda and Richard

Chapter Twenty-Three

COACHING

I am often asked to compare tennis today with the tennis and players of 60 years ago. A dangerous task. Without doubt, the inner drive and ambition to be the best appears in every generation, regardless of money, but there are differences. For me, the biggest change in the professional game is the strength and depth in the tournaments of today. The game has become truly worldwide. Players from countries that did not have tournaments 60 years ago are now winning major titles. I find this astonishing.

Technically, two obvious changes are the two-handed backhand, and the shifted forehand grip that produces more topspin. If only I could have used a two-handed backhand myself. Nick Kyrgios, the Australian Davis Cup player, has reintroduced the long-forgotten under-arm serve. A show-stopper and an unexpected yet effective tactic. Recently the men's game has seen an increased use of the one-handed backhand, which is a more attractive and versatile shot.

Equipment has improved beyond recognition. Gone are the wooden rackets, strung with gut, if you were a senior, and with nylon for juniors. These days, the pros have their rackets re-strung often on a daily basis. Re-stringing our wooden rackets might have happened two or three times a year. Dunlop Green Flash canvas shoes were worn on all surfaces – hard, clay and grass. There was no selection of soles that might grip better.

Sometimes players wore socks over their shoes to avoid slipping if the grass was damp. For ankle support we relied on our woolly ankle socks. Sadly, progress means there are no more boxes of six white balls that were once kept refrigerated on the Centre Court during the Championships. These boxes were simple to open, compared with the air-tight metal cans of today. Now, it's the drinks that are kept refrigerated.

The current circuit has increased dramatically, with both senior and junior tournaments happening 52 weeks of the year. Not all the initiatives are attractive. I find on-court coaching, for the Women's Tour, a distraction. Logically, it seems unnecessary for coaches to go on court at the change of ends to talk to their pupils during a match, especially when the coach looks more animated and keener than the pupil. Off-court coaching has been a vague area for many years, with signals between coach and player not allowed and not always secret. But despite this, I much enjoy following the tour on TV.

Two of the Grand Slam titles, the US Open and the Australian Open, used to be on grass but have now switched to hard courts. Hard courts are easier to maintain and have a truer bounce. Hence, this surface has become more popular worldwide. However, I believe, it is tougher on the joints, and players appear far more prone to strains, with much concern for the long-term health of their careers. Speaking for myself, I believe in the genetic luck of the draw or was playing on a grass surface more forgiving? I have no proof, but I certainly have no problems from the neck down and now, aged 81, I still enjoy 18 holes of golf with the same knees, hips, elbows, and back that I had when I played tennis! Hard courts have also seen the evolution of a baseline game that can be manufactured to perfection. I watch in awe the power, consistency, and accuracy of the players today. Ground shots take away the confidence of anyone brave enough to go near the net, except, of course, for my role model, Roger Federer. But never say never. There will always be changes. I still think back to the serve-and-volley game of the good-looking Pete Sampras. He was once labelled boring because his serve was so good. He reflected that no one appreciated the hours of practice it took to achieve his success, including changing his double-handed backhand to a single style, and not forgetting his trademark introduction of the slam dunk. This was a huge leap in the air while moving towards the net to smash a high ball. It took dramatic flair and risk.

The clay courts in Europe have always had a reputation for long rallies and high-bouncing balls. This tactic of high balls has not changed, but the players are more physically prepared than 60 years ago, although for me, patience on clay courts is still the winner. Nowadays, the clay-court season in Europe provides an opportunity for more variety, and to explore the width and depth of the court, especially if you are Spanish and left-handed, à la Nadal. Wimbledon completes these contrasts with the challenge of its traditional grass-court surface.

Undoubtedly, the game has been enhanced by Hawk-Eye, the electronic line judge. The suspense of waiting for a ball's final landing spot is nail-biting. Was the ball in or out? This is displayed for all to view. The tie-break, an innovation introduced in the 1970s, can also be a tear-jerker. It adds more suspense to a match with often dramatic results. Fred Perry always said: "To serve a double fault in a tie-break is fatal."

As the game became globally televised, it encouraged the placing of chairs for players to sit on at the change of ends. This gave the TV cameras a chance to focus on the players when they sat down, with close-ups of them changing their tops and drinking bottles of who-knows-what. Sitting down for two or three minutes makes the matches longer, despite giving the public time to savour the excitement. The backlash of this time taken adds to the duration of the match, though not necessarily in playing time.

The extension of a singles match can affect the decision of the top players to enter other events. My one sentimental comparison with 60 years ago is missing the top names playing doubles and mixed events, as well as singles.

My wish list would definitely include seeing my service speed displayed on Centre Court, although I know I would have wanted to beat the machine! I have suggested that the number of double faults be displayed as well! It is good news to have a clock that checks the time taken between points of play. Delays were called 'stalling' in my era – an age-old tactic to keep your opponent waiting by changing a racket, tying a shoelace, and now, the dreaded toilet break. Even medical time-outs are viewed with suspicion. Gamesmanship will always be intimidating. Fred Perry told me that he would comb his hair in front of the shared dressing room mirror before going on court. He made sure his opponent could hear when saying in a loud voice: "I would not like to be playing me today."

The question I most often get asked is: 'What age should a child start to play tennis?' The professional game has seen tennis become a promising career with financial rewards. This view of the game can influence how soon parents might encourage their children to take up the sport. Some professionals will say: "Start in the pram!" Speaking from personal experience, I was nine when I had my first lesson. I realise that was 70 years ago, but I have seen talented youngsters today bored and burnt out at 12 and 13, an age when they should be flourishing. In the US, Little Mo, Maureen Connolly, the Grand Slam Champion, had what is now an outdated dilemma, aged 10. She was a left-hander. Her coach said she could never be a champion as a left-hander. She was determined enough to hit hundreds and hundreds of balls against a wall to become a right-handed player. At 19, she won four Grand Slams in a year. As a coach myself, I wish I could give advice that taking up tennis, at a certain age, would make a champion. But, that is impossible! I believe it matters not at what age you start, but how you start. Another important lesson is to remember quality matters more than quantity. It is possible to be on court for hours but not benefit as much as a purposeful, shorter length of time. Children normally want to join in family hobbies and activities, be it sport, music or dance. This is a natural beginning. Avoiding a normal childhood by specialising at a young age, rings alarm bells. A childhood cannot be replaced. As an optimist, I would never say never, however impossible that dream may look. There will always be someone who takes an original and different route. Advising which grip, what size racket, which style, how much to compete and how much coaching, depends on the child. Tennis is an individual game. What suits one pupil might not work for another. My basic advice is to let the child be the enthusiast, with someone, be it a parent or a coach, to help with opportunities.

Success cannot be guaranteed. It is a parental balancing act of encouraging a passion without overloading the talent. Tennis is not an easy game. Billie Jean King used to quote: "If tennis is easy, why aren't all those people who are walking up and down Oxford Street playing it competitively?" I discovered it is hard to get a balance with my own daughters who wanted to play tennis. I was determined they would not grow up and tell their friends about their awful tennis mother who had made them practise every day. Consequently, they did not play very much and were disappointed to discover their friends played more than they had. Very hard to get it right.

On one occasion, a parent from my elder son's school rang to ask if he, Nigel, then aged 16, would mind giving their promising son some tennis practice during the summer term. I was told he had spent his Easter holidays at the Harry Hopman Tennis Academy in the US. I replied that of course Nigel would not mind, but he did not play tennis!

Although the professional game offers tempting financial rewards, we only see the success stories. Players growing up in this era know no different, and thrive on the opportunity to provide themselves with material advantages. When I am asked if I wonder about the money I might have made if I was playing tennis today, I can honestly say that prize money is not what I think about in my daily life. It is not on my shopping list. I quite simply felt lucky to do something I was good at.

When the unexpected happens, we all want to know how and why. Nothing could have been more unlikely than the staggering win of Emma Raducanu in New York. She caught the imagination of the whole world of sport, not just tennis, when she won the US Grand Slam title aged 18. Everyone wanted to watch Emma. We all loved her and her refreshing personality. Her game is based on wonderful timing, not a talent that can be coached. She lit up the court, especially when she spoke so generously to the TV and press after her matches. It was a fairytale, and proof that miracles can happen. Emma had to win three rounds of qualifying for entry into the main event where she won the title without losing a set. Astonishing.

Although our lives were different, there is nothing different about being 18, like Emma, when winning a Grand Slam. Regardless of the changes in equipment, surfaces – and money, of course – 18 is emotionally young. It is not grown up. Going to university at that age is a learning experience and another stage of life. There is no quick route to maturity for tennis players. The difference between Emma and me at 18 is the elevated status she now finds herself in, with little chance of catching up on knowledge of the Women's Tennis Association and its tour overnight. In contrast, I wanted the drama of being good young, and was already Top 5 in the world, having been on the circuit for two years. After Lottie Dod, a Wimbledon winner at 15, my heroine was Maureen Connolly. She won the US Nationals at 16 in

Coaching keen youngsters
at Braeside, my old school.
I enjoyed giving some of
my knowledge and
enthusiasm back

1951, followed by three Wimbledon Championships in 1952 to 1954, plus four Grand Slams in one calendar year. I wanted to emulate her career.

The age limit of 16 for senior tournaments was dropped in the 1980s. This enabled tennis prodigies to be on tour earlier, with money in the professional game an attraction. The big names of Jennifer Capriati, Andrea Jaeger, Anna Kournikova and Tracy Austin were able to enter Grand Slam events at 14. Not all the youngsters wanted or could sustain the intensity of the senior tour, so the age limit was reinstated to 16 in the 1990s. Since then, Coco Gauff is the youngest star to play at Wimbledon in 2019. Martina Hingis, the Swiss sensation (named after Martina Navratilova) won Wimbledon aged 16 in 1997, so there is always the possibility of a dynamic youngster becoming a champion, but not someone so unknown as Emma Raducanu. It will be tough for Emma, being expected to win. She is no longer the underdog. There will be many talented opponents with more experience waiting to play her.

Being more personal, I remember at 18 noticing boys! Tennis legend Chris Evert was engaged to Jimmy Connors at 19 when she won her first Wimbledon title in 1974. In her favour, Emma has known the discipline of achieving two A-levels which adds to her incredible story, but she has much to navigate. It will be hard to beat her success of 2021. Who could? But she has much to look forward to and can be proud of giving women's tennis such a tonic in 2021.

Chapter Twenty-Four

FINAL THOUGHTS

The final chapter is just that: final thoughts, final memories and final stories. Ever the optimist at 81, I tell myself: "Don't think, just do! Wait, and you wait for ever." These words stem from my coaching with Norman long ago. Writing has always been a hobby. When the children were young, I told them stories, through catchy verses, to pass the time on car journeys and at bedtime, and I have written some children's tennis books about a tennis player called Dilly. A memoir has been a very different experience, mainly because it has been a weird project to read the correspondence Mother kept that I had never seen before. I have to admit it has been emotional at times as it has involved a few thousand letters from my heyday and taken me four years to complete.

My proudest moment was in April 2011, when I was voted the 'happiest person in the country.' With this characteristic no doubt shared by many other contenders, I was glad to be recognised because I am happy! But how I was selected is a mystery. It was a government promotional survey, when David Cameron became Prime Minister. All my friends, family and even their pets were happy, so I felt lucky to be singled out.

Pride marks many special occasions in my life. It was a lifetime honour to receive an MBE from the Queen at Buckingham Palace in November 2001. It could not have happened at a better time. The brown envelope arrived just as I was taking Gerry to Ipswich hospital for his weekly session of chemotherapy for bowel cancer. I thought the envelope might contain a parking fine or a speeding ticket, which would have been far more upsetting to Gerry than his chemotherapy appointment. So, I put it to one side until we got home. Naturally, we were overjoyed to read the notice of my MBE when I finally opened the envelope.

Arranging to receive my award had to be planned around Gerry's seven months of chemo. He was allowed two weeks off from his treatment to prepare for the occasion. Going to Buckingham Palace gave the ceremony a touch of history. The behind-the-scenes precision of the organisation made me feel like a 'royal' myself. Stepping forward to meet the Queen at Buckingham Palace was more than I ever expected in my life. She talked about my radio commentary again. I can't remember our conversation word for word, but I was thrilled to exchange a few words with the Queen herself.

Afterwards, there were photographs with Gerry and my sons, Nigel and Richard, who were guests. The day was tinged with relief that Gerry had managed to be there and we celebrated at The Savoy with lunch.

Gerry was strong and determined as he recovered from bowel cancer. Whenever he was asked how he was, he always responded that he was just getting over a touch of flu. Having been evacuated during the war, aged four, to Blewbury in Oxfordshire, he only saw his parents once a year for five years during that time. This is unimaginable today, but it seemed to have given him an in-built strength. I would describe him as a kind, loyal and loving husband, someone who could not try harder to get everything right and so often get it wrong. Life was never dull. Making a cup of tea, he would invariably turn off the fish tank. The fish tank waterpump plug was next to the kettle. The fish died, but he still fed them. He always kept a jar of penny coins insisting that if he looked after the pennies, the pounds would take care of themselves. That never happened. One heart-wrenching after-noon, when we thought we had lost our new puppy, Womble, Gerry drove around Aldeburgh for a couple of hours looking for him. We thought Womble was a goner – only to find he was asleep on the back seat.

I know Gerry would agree that going to a wedding in more recent years was the last straw. He had an obsession about getting the car washed when we were going out. On this occasion we were dressed in our wedding attire and were pressed for time in getting away. Exasperated, I said: "We can go to the wedding or have the car washed. We can't do both." Despite me driving, Gerry insisted on getting the car washed! We stopped at a garage in Martlesham near Ipswich. It was a hot day. Gerry got a coin for the automatic car wash but by now I was too cross to speak as I drove into the bay. In my anger, I had not closed the car windows. The first two buckets of water came straight through both windows. Automated car windows can take a long time to close, so the second shower followed as well. That diluted my tears. Marriage can be challenging, but I can't say my hair or my outfit looked their best after that.

Acknowledgement comes in often unexpected ways. I was proud and overwhelmed to be awarded an Honorary Doctorate from the University of East Anglia in Norwich, and flattered to become a Governor of Haileybury College in Hertfordshire. Not long after my award was announced, I was at a dinner with friends when, as a teaser, I asked if they could guess who they thought would be receiving an honorary degree as a Doctor of Law. They could not think who it was, and suggested several appropriate names. When I said it was me, there was a deafening silence before someone said, tongue-in-cheek: "I do hope you will make your acceptance speech in Latin."

Putting my robes on at the presentation was a strange moment. I thought: 'Is this really me? Or was I a fraud being transformed into an academic?' Lining up to receive my doctorate, I followed an important archaeologist who had made a new discovery. When it was my turn, I felt embarrassed as I walked onto the stage to make a short speech. I wondered how I compared as a tennis player but I need not have worried. My fellow recipients were as interested in my career as I was in theirs. We were all different, but had contributed to Suffolk in various ways. Celebrating together will always have a special meaning to me and my life in Suffolk.

Life also felt purposeful when I was invited to be a Governor of Haileybury where both my husband and son had been pupils. My husband always talked fondly of his boxing days at the school but I can understand why it is banned today, although currently boxing is a popular training drill for men and women. It was a privilege to be involved in Education and the responsibilities of running a school. Haileybury is now co-educational, supporting girls and boys. It was rewarding to play a part in encouraging the girls' sport and to see the girls flourish.

Words cannot describe how thrilled I was to be given the Freedom of the City of London in 2011, following in Father's footsteps in 1947. If only he knew. Going to the Guildhall gave me an awesome sense of the history of the City of London and the importance of its Lord Mayor. I became part of that history for a day, which was especially apt as I was a Londoner and honoured to be recognised on that occasion. It was beyond special for me to receive the same award as my father who I admired so much.

Family is what I treasure most. Happily married to Gerry for 53 years, we had four children: two boys and two girls. Living in Woodford Green, the children did not know much about Wimbledon when they were little. When Richard and Amanda appeared on the TV programme *Whose Baby?* in the 1980s, a panel had to guess their famous parent. Richard, aged 6, was asked if I was in politics? He smiled and said: "Yes." Amanda, aged 4, nodded in agreement. This successfully confused the celebrity panel. No mention of Wimbledon or tennis.

Richard is happily married with three boys and a successful career as a surveyor in Cambridge. Our elder son, Nigel, sailed round the world in the Chay Blyth British Steel Challenge. He worked hard to raise the money, and maintained he entered the race to avoid Christmas at home with my party games. I am sure that's not true. Caroline and Amanda went to Cambridge University and both captained their respective Blues Tennis Teams. Caroline now works for a leading law firm in London. Amanda played in the Federation Cup in 2021, now renamed the Billie Jean King Cup. She was ranked No.2 in Britain, and played twice at Wimbledon. In her first round of the Championship, she had match point against Sesil Karatantcheva. It was nerve-wracking and heart-breaking to watch. She lost when her winning volley went out on match point. I played every point. It was never easy for Amanda to be compared with her mum. I thought she was brilliant, but she was not convinced. She now teaches English in a secondary school.

My own parents continued to enjoy tennis long after I stopped playing and took their annual holiday to watch the Eastbourne Tournament. Talking with Mother not long before she passed away, I plucked up the courage to ask her why she never showed me any sympathy. She replied: "It would not have done you any good." No more, no less. I dared not ask if it was worth a try. That was Mother. She knew I knew she did her absolute best.

Life was not without dramas. In 1984, Caroline was seriously injured when she went through a glass door; Richard fell off a chair breaking his jaw; Gerry had the first of three hip replacements. Never a nurse, there were many medical setbacks when my tennis training stepped in: "Keep on, keeping on." That's all we can do.

Yet tennis still led to unexpected surprises. I took part in an advert for Daz – 'Your Whites are Whiter than White' (Mother would have liked that). It was filmed at the Tennis Academy of the late Lew Hoad in Mijas, Spain, where his wife Jenny came to watch.

'Flora Tastes Better than Butter' saw the whole family having a picnic in Epping Forest, making sandwiches with Flora. Trying to make the children look as if they were enjoying their sandwiches was not easy, and a different treat. My work for BBC Radio helped when I became a speaker for Foyles Literary Luncheon Club. This involved travelling the length and breadth of the country, delivering my talk about tennis, 'Then and Now', at ladies' luncheons, twice a week. After 10 years, life was changing and the younger generation were working, not lunching. Slowly the luncheon club circuit faded, but it had been a job I enjoyed and fitted in easily with family life.

In 1994, Norman Kitovitz died of cancer aged 70. With a grave diagnosis, he was stoical and brave. Six weeks after having his right arm removed, he travelled alone by Tube to Woodford Green for lunch with the family. He refused all help and was his usual upbeat self. No soul-searching. No complaints. Later, I visited him in the Royal Trinity Hospice in Clapham, where he was terminally ill. I sat next to his bed. He tried to be cheerful. I wanted to say: "Please, don't." I could see it was too much for him. The vicar arrived and suggested that Norman sat in the garden where he might feel better. Norman turned to me and said: "Christine, can you tell the vicar I want to feel better before I sit in the garden?" His outlook and humour never changed. I did not see Norman again, but his advice and philosophy are indelibly printed in my memory.

One of his last stories was about being a guinea pig for the medics who treated him at a London hospital. He agreed to be examined by medical students who were training to become surgeons. Their test was to diagnose what was wrong with Norman. His right arm had been removed six weeks earlier, and the wound was still raw. But he also had a problem with two fingers on his remaining arm which were bent. Of the six students who examined him, not one recognised that he had lost his right arm, but diagnosed his bent fingers in detail. Norman thought this amusing and wondered if those students would be passing their exams. Would they really become surgeons? He also smiled when he received a box of three bars of soap for his time and contribution to medical knowledge.

In 1963, the Torch Trophy Trust Charity was formed. The late Commander Bill Collins, who had organised the 1948 London Olympic Torch relay, had the idea of recognising volunteers in sport who gave up their time to help, without ever seeing their name in lights. He invited me to join the Board of Trustees when it started, and I was there for 50 years, the longest-serving trustee. We held an annual reception in London to where 20 recipients travelled, from all over Great Britain, to receive their awards from a member of the Royal family. Prince Philip and Prince Charles attended twice. Our President, Bobby Charlton, welcomed the guests and I would read the citations. Every year it was humbling to see how much this recognition meant to the unsung heroes.

Princess Alexandra agreed to present the awards in 2001. For the first time I was given a duty connected with the Royal Visit. These duties were much in demand. I was to ask Princess Alexandra if she wanted to use the ladies' room. What a thrill to have a job to do at last! Before the ceremony, the Manager of the Army and Navy Club where our function was held, directed me to Room 319. This was to be made available for the Princess. He took me up in the lift to the third floor. Getting out of the lift, we turned left, and then right, down a corridor to Room 319. Fatally, the

Manager then handed me the key to Room 319.

When the Royal party arrived, I put the key in my handbag on a chair behind me and stood ready to receive our guests. Tension mounted as my moment arrived. I stepped forward and asked Princess Alexandra if she cared to go to the ladies' room. When she said: "Yes", I tried to look casual, not nervous like I felt. Remembering my instructions, we walked to the lift with her Lady-in-Waiting and an Aide. Chatting as we travelled up to the third-floor was easy. Getting out of the lift, my legs turned to jelly when I realised I did not have the key to Room 319. It was in my handbag downstairs. Acute embarrassment are the only words to match the situation. I felt it a calamity. Which it was. My immediate reaction was to apologise profusely. I wondered if Princess Alexandra could 'hang on whilst I fetched the key', but I could not ask. I waved to the Royal Party as I went back down in the lift to retrieve the key. We did find Room 319, and all was resolved, but that was my last duty. I wonder why! Writing to thank the Torch Trophy Trust for her wonderful evening, Princess Alexandra added a PS: 'Please send my good wishes to Christine Truman.' Some welcome encouragement indeed.

Sadly, the Torch Trophy Trust was wound up in 2019. Professional sport took over where we left off. Volunteers were becoming few and far between, but the BBC continues to recognize unsung heroes in their annual Sports Personality of the Year Awards.

Percy, a cocker spaniel, has kept me active. Although I am a fan of Jane Fonda and Joan Collins in their eighties, I do not try and compete with their exercise routines in Lycra and leotards, I just press on, doing my breaststroke in the North Sea. This is now known as wild swimming, but I am not wild about it in the winter. Playing golf helps towards regular exercise, always hoping for that elusive hole-in-one.

Looking back on the injuries and afflictions that are inevitable in a sportsperson's life, I realise my eye condition might have been significant, though it never seemed to be an impediment for my younger self. As it happens, I needed to see an eye specialist five years ago as I had a cyst on my eyelid. My appointment was made with Dr Jonathan C P Roos, who was then a Consultant Ophthalmic Surgeon at Ipswich Hospital. When we met, he asked what I did. "I used to play tennis," I said. When he discovered who I was and what I had achieved, he remarked that this was very 'British' of me.

After an examination he concluded: "Christine's vision in the left eye is so poor that she cannot make out even the top line of the vision chart." A condition that existed since my ninth birthday. My eyes were structurally sound, but I had a defect. He continued: "With a tennis ball flying at her at 120mph, Christine Janes would have had to guess where it was in space. And, with her field of view coming from only one eye, at times she may not have seen it in her left peripheral field of vision." Very generously he concluded: "This begs the question: if she was this good with one eye and no depth-perception, how much better might she have been without a disability? It is arguably the case that Christine Janes is one of – if not the – most innately talented players in the history of the sport." An unexpected, if late, acclamation. This does not change anything – but Jonathan's concluding diagnosis had an outcome that made me smile. I wish I had known this in Australia in 1960.

Encouraging tennis has long been my passion, and a lasting interest has been my involvement with tennis in Suffolk. It is pleasing to be President of the Suffolk LTA, and the popular Framlingham Tennis Tournament, also Felixstowe, Thorpeness, and Aldeburgh Tennis Clubs, not forgetting Woodford Wells Club, which is linked to my Essex roots.

Regenerating Thorpeness Country Club and the Aldeburgh Tennis Club would not have been possible without the generosity of Guy Heald in Thorpeness, and The Foundation for Sport and the Arts from Lord Grantchester, which enabled the Aldeburgh Council to resurface the local tennis courts. Both venues have seen tennis become popular once again and, with increased membership, they continue to flourish.

One of my favourite memories is associated with being a tennis coach to Aldeburgh Primary School pupils. Each year the top class would move on to their senior school in the next town, but I often see some of my former pupils in Aldeburgh.

One morning a former pupil called out: "Hello, Mrs Janes!" I responded and asked how his tennis was getting on. He looked surprised and replied: "It's going really well now I have a proper coach." Not the answer I expected! I thought I was a proper coach! In my next decade, my aim is to do better.

"Miss Truman to serve."

It seemed like a strange echo. I was on Centre Court, in my whites, racket ready. That familiar green turf looked immaculate, hardly touched. The white lines were there. Just as they were when I was 16. But this time no ball boys, no humming crowd, not even an umpire. The Championships had been cancelled because of coronavirus.

But here I was, about to serve. Extraordinary.

In the midst of a pandemic, for a week in August 2020, The All England Lawn Tennis Club broke with tradition and Centre Court and Court One were made available for club members. On a wonderful August day, one of the best that summer, I prepared to serve in a game of doubles with my daughters, Caroline and Amanda, and a friend, Suzanne Marland. I was still holding a racket at 79, 63 years after I first stepped onto the hallowed grass. I felt very conscious of the luck of the draw in my life. Afterwards, we would celebrate with a socially distanced Wimbledon champagne lunch in the Pagoda, the original competitor's restaurant that I used in 1957.

For a moment, my family shared this stage, thrilled at playing on the most sacred court in the world of tennis. I was once again where I belonged: on Centre Court, the court of Champions, where it all began a lifetime ago. This time, for once, as I hit the ball, winning didn't matter.

Receiving my MBE in 2001

Receiving my MBE, with Gerry, Nigel and Richard
at Buckingham Palace

With Gerry and Sir Stanley Rous at a Torch Trophy Trust function

With Sir Bobby Charlton, chairman of the Torch Trophy Trust

Receiving the Freedom of the City of London, 2011

Wild swimming in the North Sea, aged 80, helps me keep fit